uzi Godson

uzi Godson is *The Times* sex and relationships expert in the
JK and is author of *The Sex Book* (Cassell) and *The Body Bible*
Penguin). In 2011 she launched **www.moresexdaily.com**,
 free resource which aims to help couples sustain sex in
ong-term relationships. The site hosts a wealth of news,
esearch and advice from guest experts and is the vehicle
`or a major new survey into sexual frequency. She lives in
London with her husband and her four daughters.

SEX COUNSEL

Suzi Godson

The Times *expert answers all your questions about Sex & Relationships*

For my husband

An Hachette UK Company
www.hachette.co.uk

First published in Great Britain in 2011 by
Cassell, a division of Octopus Publishing Group Ltd
Endeavour House
189 Shaftesbury Avenue
London
WC2H 8JY
www.octopusbooks.co.uk

ISBN 978-1-84403-695-0

A CIP catalogue record for this book is available from the British Library

Printed and bound in the UK

10 9 8 7 6 5 4 3 2 1

The author and publisher cannot accept liability from any loss, damage or injury
incurred as a result (directly or indirectly) of the advice or information contained
in this book or the use or application of this book. It should not be considered as
a replacement for professional medical treatment; a physician should be consulted
in all matters relating to health and especially in relation to any symptoms that
may require diagnosis or medical attention.

Publishing Director: Stephanie Jackson
Manging Editor: Clare Churly
Editorial Assistant: Stephanie Milner
Art Director: Jonathan Christie
Design: MDesign
Production Manager: Peter Hunt

Contents

Introduction

It is more than a decade since the *Independent on Sunday* newspaper hired me to write the UK's first ever broadsheet sex column. It was a daring move and the newspaper was promptly reported to the Press Complaints Commission. Fortunately for me, the charge of obscenity was dismissed and my column, 'S is for Sex' ran unchallenged for several years. By the time Carrie Bradshaw had fully penetrated the British psyche even *The Times* was ready for sex, and in 2004 I decamped and began writing the column that is now known as 'Sex Counsel'.

By 2009, *The Times* was online and the volume of enquiries about sex had increased exponentially as a result, however the nature of the questions had changed. There were notably fewer mentions of erectile dysfunction because Viagra and its competitors Levitra and Cialis were already so well known. And thanks to online shopping I got fewer and fewer enquiries from shy post-menopausal women who wanted to know how to go about buying a vibrator. More recently, the contraction of the economy and the expansion of the internet has generated a tsunami of correspondence about the stress of unemployment and associated issues such as boredom, porn use and chatroom infidelity.

It is not just reader's questions that have changed over the years, the editorial goalposts have also shifted considerably. In the early days of the 'Sex Counsel' column the words 'vagina' and 'erection' were routinely snipped from my copy, but some years later a certain male editor clearly favoured letters from spankers and swingers. More recently, my columns have been subject to 'The Croissant Test', an indeterminate measure which estimates the likelihood of a question causing a *Times* reader to choke on their breakfast.

It is a test I frequently fail because sex is such a messy, complex and controversial subject and there is no polite, one-size-fits-all solution to the knots that individuals and couples tie themselves into. When two people start a relationship they take with them a predictable, almost universal, set of hopes and aspirations, which usually includes the dream of a happy ending. In reality, the minute they form a couple they begin to create their own unique narrative, a script which is driven by their personalities, their experiences, their sexual history and more often than not the trolley of monogrammed emotional baggage that they have each dragged into the relationship.

The letters I receive are a window into the human condition: love, sex, birth, jealousy, divorce, death, not to mention gimp hoods and dressing up in women's clothing. Sex touches every aspect of our lives. It is physical, emotional, psychological and political. It can be the very best and the very worst of our experiences, and despite millions of Google pages dedicated to the subject, it continues to perplex us all.

This book represents a small selection of the hundreds of letters that I have answered over the years. As a collection, they create a fascinating snapshot of the complexities of sexual relationships, and they remind us that the way we live may have changed unrecognizably, but the way we love hasn't changed at all.

—*Suzi Godson, 2011*

1.

Anxiety, obsession & the inadequacies of telepathy

I don't know if I am good in bed so I am not confident and almost scared about having sex with new partners. I am 22 and I have had lots of boyfriends but none sticks around. I wonder if it is because I am bad at sex. Can you tell if you are doing something wrong?

If it is any consolation, being scared about sex is bang on trend. The heart-throb Robert Pattinson recently admitted that 'when it comes to the opposite sex [he] lacks confidence and feels very self-conscious'.

Apparently raunchy rock star Lady Gaga also has 'no confidence when it comes to men', and even glamour model Jennifer Ellison is 'too scared to have sex … outside'. Why so much insecurity? I blame porn myself. Sex never used to be a comparative sport – people just got on with it behind closed doors – but with one in three children now accessing online pornography by the age of 10, it is becoming increasingly difficult for young people to gauge what constitutes normal sexual behaviour.

While researching for her book *Pornland: How Porn Has Hijacked Our Sexuality*, Dr Gail Dines, a professor of sociology and women's studies at Wheelock College, in Boston, discovered that the more porn young men watch, the more they want 'porn sex'.

This is because they become used to industrial-strength sex and it makes everything else look boring or uninteresting.

Another study, carried out in Swedish genitourinary clinics by Tanja Tydén and Christina Rogala, of the Department of Public Health and Caring Sciences, examined the impact of pornography on the sexual behaviour of 16-year-old males. Of those questioned, 99 per cent had consumed pornography and 53 per cent felt that pornography had an impact on, or had inspired, their sexual behaviour.

As an example, about half of the group had anal intercourse (70 per cent more than once) but only 17 per cent always used a condom in this situation.

If porn has created unrealistic levels of sexual expectation, at the other end of the spectrum it has also created great insecurity. 'Why don't I look like that? Why don't I respond like that? Why can't I bring myself to do that?' It is difficult for anyone to enjoy sex if they are fretting about their 'performance' and, needless to say, the more a person worries, the less likely they are to experience orgasm.

That cycle of anxiety is the main reason why women who fear failure decide to fake orgasm. They want their partner to think that they are good in bed so they moan a little white lie, but then they discover that 'faking it' has compounded rather than alleviated their sexual difficulties, because their partner then believes that they can have a rip-roaring orgasm after no foreplay and two minutes of vaginal intercourse.

The only consolation is that despite the fact that the porn industry has larger revenues than Microsoft, Google and Apple combined, most people eventually work out that real-life sex is a warm, wet, messy interaction between two people who are willing to risk baring their souls, and pretty much everything else, because they believe that in return they will receive love, affection and, hopefully, an orgasm.

Unfortunately, the level of maturity required to achieve such intimacy and honesty rarely materializes in men under the age of 25, so you may have to put up with several more years of non-stick dating before you find a keeper.

Use the time well. Stop worrying and give yourself permission to enjoy kissing a few frogs. They don't bite and, one day, one of them will turn out to be a prince.

I was married for ten years to a man who had little interest in sex. We're divorced but my self-esteem is still low. Is he abnormal or is there something wrong with me?

Though you would probably find comfort in a response that explained your ex-husband's indifference to sex as abnormal, I don't think there is much point in you dwelling on his problems. Divorce leaves everyone feeling shattered but, if you want to move on, it is your part in the equation that you need to understand, not his. There are a hundred possible reasons for his iciness but none of them will explain why you allowed yourself to be emotionally abused by him for so long or what you were trying to escape when you married him.

As an objective observer, it's difficult to avoid the conclusion that your low self-esteem is not a recent phenomenon. In fact, I would suggest that you had a low opinion of yourself when you first met him. If his interest in you was a rare affirmation in a world of negativity then it is hardly surprising that you grasped what you thought was an opportunity for happiness. You projected your hopes and desires on to him and he didn't live up to your expectations. But just how realistic were those expectations? When we want something badly enough we can convince ourselves of anything, so you may have excused his initial reticence as shyness or interpreted his coldness as strength. Or perhaps you just recognized his type. Did his cruel disinterest touch a childish nerve in you? Whatever your motivations, I have no doubt that you married your ticket to the future with genuine optimism in your heart.

It probably took a couple of years for you to fully comprehend the problems and I'm sure you then made every effort to resolve them but the realization that things would never change should, in normal circumstances, have really begun to sink in after three or four years. One would have expected you to consider your options at that point, but a decade later you were still hanging in and, as you don't even say that you divorced him, I suspect that he was the one to finish the relationship in the end.

There is no doubt that your ex-husband has problems but the relationships we choose mirror only how we feel about ourselves. He treated you badly but, by staying with him, you allowed it. He had no respect for you, but the fact that you didn't leave suggests that you had even less respect for yourself. The experience has left you feeling angry, impotent and humiliated but now that the relationship is over you have a chance to put the past behind you and do what you should have done ten years ago. Rescue yourself. Stop analysing his inadequacies and address your own issues.

Start by investing in your emotional well-being. Alternative therapies like meditation or yoga may be beneficial but if you want to establish a more robust opinion of yourself you probably need to go back and explore how your self-esteem became so fragile in the first place. Cognitive behavioural therapy is a remarkably effective way of understanding the feelings that undermine happiness and confidence, finding constructive ways of controlling anxiety and changing negative behaviour. Contact the British Association of Behavioural and Cognitive Psychotherapies for more information.

Finally, remember that you can't have a functional relationship with anyone if you don't have one with yourself.

My wife has always kept the house clean, but recently she has become obsessive and it is having an impact on our sex life. She will rarely have sex because it's 'dirty' – after we have sex, she insists that we both have a shower and sticks the sheets in the washing machine the next day. How can I make her relax?

As one who has always been domestically challenged, I see a lot of upsides to your wife's behaviour. Clean house. Fresh linen on the bed. Fastidious personal hygiene. However, I also see that your wife is nursing some sort of obsessive compulsive disorder (OCD), and that's obviously too high a price to pay for a tidy anything. Approximately 1.5 million people in the UK have full-blown OCD, but as many as 25 per cent of the population show milder symptoms. For example, I always thought that my husband was merely an uptight Virgo, but then I began to notice how he obsessively touches the walls and triple-locks the front door.

Similarly, David Beckham can't relax unless the contents of his fridge are in perfect formation, and when he sleeps in a hotel room he moves all the furniture so that it lines up. It's weird, but not weird enough to interfere with daily life, so myself, and Posh presumably, simply raise our eyes to heaven and let them get on with it.

People with OCD nearly always know that their behaviour is abnormal, but they can be reluctant to admit that their rituals are in any way compromising because they don't want to be labelled mentally ill.

Instead, they carry on lining up the Coke cans, washing their hands or checking that the door is locked, because that is the only way they know how to calm their anxieties. And because no one likes to upset their partner, you, me and

Posh enable the madness by giving up on sex, triple locking or trying not to disturb the fridge or the furniture.

It can be difficult to diagnose OCD because it manifests in so many different ways, though contamination fears and issues surrounding sex are among the most common symptoms in women. And the two things are often linked. Women who have developed acute anxiety about germs in the home feel the same about bodily secretions, and because they find the idea of sex frightening, disgusting, or both, they go out of their way to avoid it. Often it is only when the non-OCD partner refuses to tolerate the strange behaviour that the sufferer is forced to address the problem, but by then it may be too late. Joel Rose, director of OCD Action, says that it takes sufferers an average of 12 years to seek help, which is nuts because 80 per cent of people with OCD can get their obsessions under control with as few as 16 sessions of cognitive behavioural therapy and/or medication.

Though you can't force your wife to seek help, you can help her to acknowledge that she has a problem. The online screening test at OCD Action is not a diagnosis but it may help her to recognize triggers. If the results of the screening point to OCD, she should call the helpline. She will need to see a doctor to get a referral for cognitive behavioural therapy on the NHS, or she can find one privately through the British Association of Behavioural and Cognitive Psychotherapies. There are also several excellent guides available on symptoms, treatments and self-help solutions.

I've met a lovely man, but I have panic attacks when he tries to make a move. I had this problem 25 years ago and gave up on sex. Am I allergic to love?

Your 25 years of self-imposed celibacy suggest something slightly more sinister than an allergy, my love, but I'm sure you know that already. Panic attacks occur when people cannot cope with certain situations and their stress manifests itself as a physical response. The symptoms of panic become fixed associations with a particular episode and sufferers, understandably, do their best to avoid putting themselves in that position again. Research carried out at the Federal University of Rio de Janeiro indicated that 50 per cent of women who suffer regular panic attacks also suffer from sexual aversion disorder, a form of panic attack that manifests specifically in relation to sexual contact. People with sexual aversion disorder may be averse to a single aspect of sex such as genital contact. Others are revolted by all sexual stimuli, even touching and kissing. The Rio study suggests that it is not sexual dysfunction, but the fear of having a panic attack that causes sexual aversion disorder.

Nearly all people suffering from it will go to heroic lengths to avoid sexual activity. Certain people have a greater hereditary predisposition to panic attacks and, inevitably, children who have a genetic tendency who also have difficult childhoods are more likely to manifest anxiety in this way in later life. Sexual abuse, rape, death, domestic violence, divorce, bad relationships, poverty or even unsatisfactory employment can bring on panic disorders, but sometimes normal life changes may trigger attacks. Finishing school or college, changing jobs, moving house or having a baby can all have a cumulatively stressful effect. You may or may not be aware of what triggered your panic but your strategy – avoidance – is surely the most common form of self-help. Though recent surveys indicate that panic disorders affect up to 18 per cent of people in the UK, an estimated 75 per cent of sufferers do not get professional help. Avoidance might be viable for someone suffering from selachophobia (fear of sharks), but you shouldn't spend your life avoiding sex.

Falling in love and establishing a sexual relationship are among the most joyous experiences. It would be tragic if fear denied you this opportunity. If this lovely man cares, he will understand your anxieties, but if the relationship is to blossom he will need to see you making a concerted effort to tackle them. The best way is through a course of cognitive behavioural therapy (CBT). The British Association for Behavioural and Cognitive Psychotherapies provides an online list of registered therapists. Or try contacting No Panic, a national charity specializing in helping people who suffer from panic attacks. CBT has an estimated 80 per cent success rate, though Colin Hammond, who founded the charity, says: 'Success with panic disorders is relative. It doesn't necessarily mean that an agoraphobic will fly to the moon, but it does mean that people can live comfortably and happily.'

After 25 years on your own, I think you deserve a little of that, don't you?

I'm a rich, OK-looking, 40-ish alpha male, yet I'm lonely. Every time I'm in bed with a woman I feel sick with nerves and can't get it up. Please help.

OK, but only if you give me your number so that I can set you up with some of my less rich, OK-looking, thirtysomething beta girlfriends when you feel better about yourself. They're lonely too. The alarm on their biological clocks has been ringing for, ooh, about five years now, so on the rare occasions when they go on a date they find themselves so sick with nerves that they are barely able to string a sentence together.

You would get on because you have a lot in common. Your shared history starts in the early Sixties. Born into a society that offered men and women both equal rights and sexual freedom, you and my girlfriends made money, made friends, made out, and made it to this age without meeting anyone that met all your requirements. It didn't matter much if you broke up with Monica, there was always Jessica or Erica. But then all your friends started taking the plunge and you began to feel less like a lucky Lothario and more like the odd man out.

The older you get the more weighted dating has become and when the stakes are high, nervousness is inevitable. When it comes to sex, this is a disaster. Male performance-anxiety is a self-fulfilling prophecy and unless you can get yourself out of the loop nothing will change. Although it is your failure to perform that is getting you down, your problem has little to do with sex. Like so many men and women of your age, somewhere on your journey from childhood to this aspirational, performance-obsessed, super-materialistic, adult world, you devalued the most important relationship in your life: the one you have with yourself. You began to gauge your personal happiness in consumer terms. Girlfriends had to meet certain criteria.

None measured up but you were incomplete without the right person. Ergo, you didn't measure up. So you wind up rich, OK-looking, 40-ish and an alpha male, but you feel inadequate because you can't find someone else to make you feel adequate.

How wrong is that? You need to step back and stop evaluating your worth in terms of looks and wealth, and start assessing who you really are, what you want out of life, what genuine attributes you appreciate in others and what you can offer in return.

You will be in good company. Throughout history great men have chosen to retreat from the material world to achieve greater understanding. Jesus spent 40 days in the wilderness preparing himself for the defining period of his life and Robert the Bruce, King of Scotland, minutely observed a spider on a cave wall before going out to defeat the English armies.

Contemplation is enormously underrated these days. Most of us go from job to job, or relationship to relationship, without missing a beat. In our haste to build and amass we leave nothing to chance or serendipity or fate. What you are doing – panic buying at the supermarket of love in the hope that you will happen on the items that you really need – is pointless. The smart shopper listens to his heart, makes a list and heads directly to the appropriate aisle. So, mull before you pull. Evaluate whether a liason has real or meaningful potential before you try to make it sexual. And when you meet someone that you believe has great qualities, tell her, and tell her that you have been lonely in the past and that you feel nervous now. Honesty, integrity and a certain degree of vulnerability? Now there's a turn-on.

A previous partner made me feel so embarrassed of my occasional farts that, at 50, I feel too self-conscious to have a relationship with a man. Help!

Everyone farts. Nelson Mandela. The Virgin Mary. Even the Queen. And although Her Majesty undoubtedly makes an effort to steer clear of baked beans before a big engagement, I'm sure she lets the occasional one slip on her jet. (Low pressure environments make gas expand, which is why aircraft usually stink by the time they reach a long-haul destination.) Since I imagine the Queen has fairly high self-esteem, she probably does what most of us would do in that situation and just laughs it off, or rather, waves it away, but I certainly don't think she would let the Duke of Edinburgh give her an earful for what is a universal bodily function.

Arguably, any woman who can allow a man to make her feel so bad about doing something so normal has got some serious issues to sort out and I can only presume that your previous partner's comments have tapped into pre-existing anxieties or feelings of shame.

A cognitive behavioural therapist would ask you to come up with convincing evidence that people who fart cannot find or keep sexual partners. Think about it. Everyone farts, so it stands to reason that it is impossible not to fart in a relationship. If this was not the case, the species would have failed to survive.

Asked the secret of a long happy marriage, one man who had been married for 40 years answered: 'Separate bathrooms.' The psychosexual therapist Jane Gibbins agrees that 'a little mystery helps to keep erotic life alive' but adds that 'the odd fart between lovers is surely just human'.

At the beginning of a relationship most men and women do their best to hold everything in as much as possible but, sooner or later, two people who are happy to suck each other's genitals generally arrive at the conclusion that jumping out of bed at three in the morning just so that they can fart in the privacy of the bathroom is unsustainable.

Though I would urge you to accept yourself as normal and find a less critical partner, if you want to boost your confidence there are a few things you can do to cut down the amount of gas that your digestive system produces. Foods linked to an increase in gas production include potatoes, onions, dark beer and red wine, and obviously anything carbonated is a no-no.

Soluble fibres (oats, peas, beans, root vegetables and citrus fruits) that aren't broken down until they enter the large intestine produce more gas than insoluble fibres (wheat, bran, whole grain and wholemeal cereals), which break down in the small intestine.

You can also help to strengthen your sphincter muscle by doing Kegel exercises to work the muscles that support your pelvic organs. To isolate these muscles try either stopping and starting the flow of urine, or inserting a finger into your vagina and trying to tighten the muscles around it. The abdominal and thigh muscles remain relaxed but you should feel your vagina and sphincter muscles tensing. Once you have located the right muscles, slowly tighten and hold them for six to eight seconds, and then relax. Do this exercise as three sets of eight to 12 contractions, two to four days a week, for up to five months, and you should see a dramatic improvement in your muscle tone, confidence and sex life.

I've been dating a fellow student for six months, but after sex he insists on sleeping alone, so he goes home. Does that mean he doesn't love me?

I had a boyfriend like that once. For the first couple of months that we were seeing each other he would come over to my place, we would make out, then we'd both go to bed together and at 3 a.m. he would climb out of bed, put on his clothes and go home. He told me that it was because he couldn't sleep if he had to share a bed and I believed him. I didn't mind that much, actually. Privacy is a vital part of conserving the mystery in any new relationship and, let's face it, there is only so long that a person can survive without breaking wind. Besides, morning has never been my best look. Panda eyes, bird's nest hair and Snoopy pyjamas were definitely reserved for long-term commitment; as for the horrifying prospect of him using the bathroom straight after me? As I said, I didn't mind him going home.

However, at a certain time in any relationship you reach a point where you have The Talk. The Talk is generally about whether or not you have a future, but it usually involves coming clean about people you haven't quite finished with, prospective love interests or general hangers-on.

When Mr 3 a.m. and I had the The Talk, he eventually confessed that he was seeing someone else. 'You're not seeing very much of her,' I pointed out, since he had been at my house almost every night since we met. He agreed, but said, as only someone equipped with a Y chromosome could, that by not actually staying the night with me he felt he wasn't really making a commitment to me and, as such, if things didn't work out between us he could go back to Miss Waiting On The Side with a clear conscience.

If he started sleeping over, he thought that the relationship would get really serious and I would expect him to be there all the time, which would freak him out; whereas waking up in his own bed gave him a sense of autonomy. It was a way of nipping intimacy in the bud and keeping me at arm's length.

I told him he could shove his autonomy where the sun didn't shine and, within a week, he was begging to leave a toothbrush in my bathroom. It was a high risk strategy, but one you might consider. Although there is a small chance that your 'boyfriend' misses his Arsenal duvet, your gut instinct is clearly telling you that something is wrong, and you should listen. I'm not suggesting that he is stringing someone else along, but his behaviour indicates that he is less committed to you than you are to him.

Whether he has issues with intimacy or doesn't want to get too involved, six months of having sex and waking up alone would ring alarm bells in any woman. If you haven't been clear with him about your concerns, it is time that you and he sat down and worked out what you both want out of this relationship. Most people avoid this kind of open discussion because they are afraid of having to reject someone or, indeed, being rejected themselves. But, if you like him and you want to move things on towards any kind of exclusive commitment, then you need to define the parameters of your relationship. And you can do this only if you talk openly to each other.

It's strange that so many of us find it easier to have sex than to talk to each other but, hey, if it was any other way, I'd be out of a job.

I have just started going out with someone and whenever we get to the bedroom, there's a lot of grabbing and rolling around and heavy breathing, but it has never actually got as far as foreplay, and certainly not sex. I don't find it sexy, and don't know how to get to the next level without explicitly asking, which I would find embarrassing, because he obviously thinks his behaviour is a turn-on.

Being too embarrassed to talk about sex has been the death of many an otherwise promising relationship. I know a guy who was too shy to mention his haemorrhoids when his brand new girlfriend started stimulating his prostate during sex. He broke up with her as soon as he regained the power of speech. Similarly, I know a girl who couldn't bring herself to tell a newish boyfriend that her period was due because he had taken her to a five star hotel for the night. The next morning it looked as if someone had been murdered and needless to say when they checked out of the hotel, they checked out of their relationship too.

Couples who can't be honest with each other about sex, probably shouldn't be having it anyway. However anyone who has ever had a relationship appreciates that it is difficult to be open, particularly at the beginning of a new relationship. In the first weeks or even months you are trying to convey the 'ideal' version of yourself and although you don't intend to present a façade, you do tailor your behaviour to impress. You put more thought into what you wear. You don't break wind. Or speak with your mouth full. You tell your best and funniest stories over dinner. And in the bedroom you pull out what you think are your best sex moves. What you don't tend to do is criticize your partner or reveal anything that might, potentially, make them think less of you.

The trouble with that kind of selective restraint is that the more you withhold, the bigger the gap between what goes on in your head, and what goes on in your bed. Right now you are harbouring doubts about his Mr Bean technique and whether you are ever going to get to third base, but if you can't tackle these relatively simple issues, I'm wondering how you are planning to broach the subjects of safe sex, condoms and contraception? I very much doubt your partner is going to address them because he sounds so inexperienced that I suspect he may have 'L' plates beneath his trousers. And if this is the case and you are too afraid to be explicit, how are you going to help him to learn the subtleties of successful stimulation?

That which cannot be discussed with clothes on, rarely becomes easier to talk about with clothes off, yet a percentage of men and women are such slaves to their own shyness that they would prefer to endure compromised sex, orgasmic inequity and even fake orgasm rather than risk the possibility that they might say the wrong thing. Don't be one of them. Despite your misgivings about his sexual style, you clearly like this guy and want to take things further, so just do it. Assertiveness is way more sexy than reticence, so next time you get him into the bedroom, throw down a pack of featherlite. Unbutton his jeans. Take your shirt off. Make it blindingly obvious that you are ready to go and then use words and actions to guide him as required. Even if he is all fingers and thumbs at the start, guys are good at following instruction. The male brain has better mathematical and spatial skills which is why men tend to be better at reading maps, building flat plan furniture and programming the DVD player. Women, on the other hand, have stronger verbal and social skills, and greater empathy, which makes them better at finding sensitive ways of addressing difficult or awkward subjects.

I haven't had sex in ages, and I now have a new boyfriend but am too embarrassed to have sex when I'm sober. Will I always feel like this?

Give yourself a break, honey. New relationships are such an exhausting combination of excitement and angst that most women would never get past first base without a bit of Dutch courage. Dating tends to happen in pubs and restaurants where alcohol is a key feature, and 'getting to know someone' is such an incredibly stressful experience that there is a genuine need for disinhibition.

Before a woman is ready to invest emotionally she needs about a million questions answered. Is he single? Is this just an opportunity for casual sex for him? Does that matter? Are we talking potential cohabitation? Or, deep breath, could he be the one? And what about kids? Is he fertile? Does he always wear a baseball hat?

That's just the stuff that runs through a woman's head at home in the bathroom, trying to work out whether her blue eyeshadow clashes with her earrings. By the time she gets to the pub for her first date she is either walking up the aisle or ready to beat him over the head with a rolling pin and there is only one legal way to disengage the inner critic intent on sabotaging her only chance of happiness. Vodka.

Romance and alcohol have been inextricably linked since time immemorial. And for good reason. The level of expectation that clutters up a woman's psyche can beat a fledgling romance to death in minutes, if it weren't for the benevolent hand of Bacardi. It is a scientific fact that alcohol temporarily makes everything, even the baseball hat, look rosy. Researchers from the Universities of St Andrews and Glasgow recently spent taxpayers' money proving that men and women who consume a moderate amount of alcohol find the faces of the opposite sex more attractive than do their sober counterparts. Consume between one and four units and the target of your affections looks 25 per cent more attractive; between four and 20 units and you run the risk of waking up next to Bubbles DeVere from *Little Britain*, and having to chew your arm off so you can get out of there before she goes in for round two.

Though you have reservations, and possibly hazy memories as to how you have arrived at this particular point, don't be too hard on yourself. Booze has served a purpose for you. You felt shy and it made you feel less so. Great. And now you have a boyfriend who obviously likes you, and you obviously like him, which is super-great. Take it from there and don't look back.

As for having sex when you are sober: this Saturday, instead of rushing home in case he sees you with your eye make-up halfway down your face, take a risk, snuggle in under his arm and say 'sod it'. When he makes love to you in the morning, sober and panda-eyed, you have taken your first tentative steps into the comfort zone, a blissed out state in which all your critical faculties are suspended indefinitely. Enjoy!

2.

Rabbits, fleshlights
& flying solo

I am 27 and have been with my boyfriend for four years but I have never been able to have an orgasm; I am very active and don't have time to spend hours masturbating so I have never been able to get beyond a certain point of arousal (legs shaking, etc). I have been to a psychosexual therapist but it didn't work. Would hypnosis help?

Hours? Heavens to Betsy, what are you doing to yourself? It is hardly surprising that you are less than enthusiastic about self-dating if you are still plodding towards tingling when the washing machine has done a full cycle. A self-induced orgasm can normally be squeezed into the time it takes to boil a kettle – if you are sufficiently aroused before you turn it on. I suspect this is where you're going wrong.

Orgasm is an involuntary reflex which can be either discouraged or encouraged. Anxiety and stress inhibit it. Arousal brings it on. If you try to pleasure your body when your brain is still engaged in a spreadsheet on household finances, you might as well give up. To achieve orgasm you need to shut down your rational brain and boot up your sensual self, and until you work out how to give yourself one, forget about having one with your boyfriend.

Thankfully, there is a range of helpful literature available to encourage you to press the right buttons. You can buy these books discreetly online (though rifling through display copies in a public bookstore brings on teenage palpitations) and they are guaranteed to heighten your arousal. Assuming you have a basic grasp of anatomy and have worked out the difference between your clitoris (about 8,000 nerve endings) and your vagina (about eight nerve endings), you can skip the sex manuals and go straight to erotic novels.

Don't be put off by the naff titles and don't expect much of a plot. Erotic fantasy is goal driven and should be viewed as a means to an end. You are simply looking for something that will give your arousal a jump start, so if *The Adventures of a Lesbian College School Girl* gets you going, disengage the prim side of your brain and just go for it. If you don't know where to begin, try the classics. *The Story of O*, by Pauline Reage, or *A Journal of Love* and *A Spy in the House of Love*, by Anaïs Nin, are a well-trodden path – but they work.

You should also invest in a decent vibrator. Buying online is anonymous and highly efficient, although a trip to a sex shop can lead to the kind of impulse purchasing that a computer screen rarely encourages. There is an enormous range of styles to choose from though the Rampant Rabbit, as seen on *Sex and the City*, is still incredibly popular, (if you type in 'sex toys for women' on a search engine, it is practically *Watership Down*) and since it offers both penetrative and clitoral stimulation it's a good entry-level model. Buy plenty of lubricant, too. It makes all the difference to solo sex.

Once you are armed and informed you are ready to try again. Turn off the phones, lock the door and let nothing or no one disturb you. Now read. Don't touch yourself or your new toys. Just read until you feel your levels of arousal building up. When you feel completely distracted by the sensations in your nether regions, apply a little lubricant and gently masturbate your clitoris while you carry on reading.

When you can't concentrate any more and your mind is brimful of fantasy, try rubbing the lubricated vibrator gently over your genitals. Keep focusing on what you are feeling and whatever it is you are fantasizing about (no matter how outrageous or out of character).

Insert the vibrator, making sure to keep the ears of the rabbit working over your clitoris. When you get to the point you have reached before (legs shaking, possibly an itchy nose), you need to break through the barriers that held you back. Keep the images in your head alive, but allow yourself to register the waves of sensation in your genitals.

When the feeling becomes more intense, go with it. Let it build up and use your pelvic-floor muscles to help squeeze the climax out. When an orgasm eventually washes over you, let everything go. Relax. And then go and put that kettle on.

I am a 33-year-old man and I find it difficult to reach an orgasm with a woman. I frequently masturbate and wonder if this is affecting my ability to climax with a partner?

In 1981, *The Hite Report on Male Sexuality* detailed the sexual habits and beliefs of 7,000 men aged between 13 and 97. One of the many insights revealed in Shere Hite's exhaustive investigation was that men find masturbation to be a more efficient and effective means of sexual release than intercourse with a partner.

The reasons they gave ranged from feeling less inhibited because there was no pressure to perform to stronger orgasms because they were completely in control of the pace and the strength of their stimulation. If Hite were to conduct the same research today, I doubt that the responses would be different.

Once a man establishes that his risk of going blind is negligible, masturbation becomes a fairly routine part of his week, sexual relationship or no sexual relationship. Though women have a tendency to read too much into the intimate relationship between a man and his right hand, it rarely causes a problem. That is unless it develops into a compulsion, or a man becomes so conditioned to his own brand of manipulation that penetrative or oral sex fails to provide him with sufficient stimulation to achieve orgasm.

Sex researchers call this phenomenon autosexual orientation. The term covers men who are reliant on a completely constant form of self-stimulation as well as those who get used to such an 'idiosyncratic' style of stimulation that they disable their ability to ejaculate during regular sex. When the sex that you have with yourself is so perfect that you can't translate it into sex with someone else, you have a problem.

Dr David Goldmeier, a sexual dysfunction expert at St Mary's Hospital, London, says: 'Some men who suffer from retarded ejaculation report that the combination of very erotic fantasies at masturbation, combined with highlevel manual friction, enable them to climax in that scenario, but that vaginal sex is not so much of a turn-on, because the man does not get the same degree of stimulation and because the woman is not as erotic as their personalized masturbatory fantasy.'

It goes without saying that you should not be in a hurry to share this information with any sexual partner. If, as you suspect, your masturbatory habits are interfering with your ability to climax, the obvious solution is to cut it out for a while and see what happens. If a period of abstinence does not solve the problem, you need to see a doctor because it could be a symptom of an underlying illness, such as diabetes, MS, nerve damage, booze. Or some kind of psychological disturbance: depression, antidepressants, fear that the vagina will grow teeth and bite off your penis.

You don't mention whether the women you have sex with

manage to achieve orgasm either, but when it comes to not coming during penetrative sex, female partners are probably the best people to talk to. A fundamental design flaw means that the most sensitive part of our sexual anatomy happens to be outside, rather than inside, our vagina, and as a result many women need additional stimulation to reach the point of no return. I suspect that a little between-the-sheets honesty would go a long way towards helping both you and the women you have sex with to have a better time in bed.

I encourage my wife of 30 years to masturbate during sex as she finds it difficult to orgasm. She doesn't want to, and claims she has never masturbated. Surely this must make her very closed to her sexual feelings. I feel selfish for reaching orgasm every time. How can I encourage her to open up more?

If your wife has been saying 'no' to your suggestion for 30 years I'd be inclined to give up on it, you know. Regardless of how beneficial you believe it would be, any woman who manages to get through the heat of adolescence, the anticipation of dating and the mundanity of marriage without ever laying a finger on herself is unlikely to break out in a sweat at menopause and decide that masturbation suddenly seems like a really great idea. Although you clearly mean well, your encouragement may actually be doing more harm than good.

Given her historic unwillingness to explore masturbation, asking her to do something that she has never done before, in front of you, and your expectations, is almost certainly asking too much. For the beginner, solo sex is a uniquely personal experience and if your wife was ever going to get to grips with it what she would need most is privacy. She might also require a biology lesson, a decent lubricant and a vibrator, but she certainly wouldn't want an audience.

The fact that your wife has never previously felt the urge to relieve an inconvenient tremor of arousal by locking the door and getting it on with herself suggests that she is indeed 'closed to her sexual feelings'. Women have to be relaxed to allow climax to occur and if your wife is anxious about orgasm, this in itself is enough to ensure that it never happens.

Female arousal is a flame that gets snuffed out or turned into a raging forest fire depending on the conditions. If a woman suppresses or feels guilty about sexual feelings, she will stop her arousal catching light. If she worries about satisfying her partner or feels uncomfortable about her sexual capabilities, her arousal might flicker dimly, but it will never get big enough to generate real heat.

Your wife's reluctance to explore her own sexuality may be a result of her upbringing or something that has happened in her past. It may be that, when you got together 30 years ago, she was inexperienced and shy, and pretended to enjoy the sex that you had together more than was really the case – and she has never felt able to tell you the truth.

Whatever the reason, it is time that you stopped badgering her and started listening to her. Somewhere inside she probably recognizes what is wrong but is worried about your reaction. So, if you really want to help her, you need to give her permission to talk openly and to assure her that whatever she says, all you want to do is to find a way for her to get more out of your sex life.

You may find that this kind of honesty is all it takes to alleviate her anxiety and help her to relax. But in order to ensure that she reaches orgasm, you will also need to slow things down because women take much longer to get aroused than men. Female orgasm is often described as 'a triumph of stimulation over inhibition' but, sadly, too many men allow their own desire to dictate the sexual pace and don't pay enough attention to their partner's sexual needs.

When this happens, many women, particularly the less sexually confident, find it too embarrassing to say anything even though their silence effectively minimizes their chances of reaching climax. A couple who want to achieve orgasmic equilibrium have to be confident enough to demand more stimulation and to tell each other if they are, or aren't, ready for intercourse.

However, in case you feel that you and your wife are the only ones who have trouble in this department, bear in mind that 75 per cent of men in partnerships always have an orgasm with their partner. Only 29 per cent of women do.

I've always had an active sex life with my husband of 19 years. But he has now acquired an artificial vagina. Does this mean he is losing interest in me?

Why does your husband need a fake vagina when he can have your real one for free? The answer is far simpler than the question. Whether it's a car, a computer console, a flat-screen plasma TV or an ultra-realistic cyberskin model of Pammy Anderson's vibrating parts, men just love gadgets, especially desirable fashion-forward gadgets that incorporate the kind of futuristic technology that generates lots of 'oohs' and 'aahs' down the pub.

Admittedly, artificial vaginas have never fallen into this category, but in 1998 a former police officer in the United States patented a 'device for discreet sperm collection'. His design for an artificial vagina cost more than $2 million to develop, but it was money well spent as the Fleshlight is now the world's bestselling sex toy for men.

It is basically an interchangeable vaginal tunnel disguised inside a – wait for it – torch. Nothing too special about that, you might say, but, unlike other sex toys, the Fleshlight is not made from latex, plastic or silicone but a patented material called Real Feel Super Skin, which has a velvety touch and is slightly lubricated. The inner sleeve of the device is available in a range of orifices; choose from vagina, anus, mouth or Super Tight Mini-Maid, which is designed, apparently, to feel more like heterosexual anal penetration (it's important to avoid gender confusion, even with sex toys).

Recently Fleshlights have incorporated celebrity porn mouldings so you can get a Vanilla DeVille or a Raven Riley labia, for example. You can also opt for a 'Stealth', which the website describes as 'perfect for dodging those embarrassing moments when questioned by customs officers about your "flashlight that doesn't turn on".' Ho, ho.

The manufacturers have marketed this product avidly, with the many journalists who were sent a freebie describing it as the 'ultimate faux vagina' and a sex toy that has 'raised the bar exponentially' for men. It even has its own YouTube slot. The great press means that sales have rocketed and thousands, nay millions, of men such as your husband, who wouldn't otherwise have dreamt of succumbing to the delights of an artificial vagina, have given this intriguing technologically advanced sex toy a chance.

Buying one isn't difficult. Your husband could even have placed an order from his desk as the Fleshlight is available from Amazon. The online bookstore sells a vast range of sex products, including vibrators.

Ever since the *Sex and the City* character Charlotte was introduced to a vibrating bunny, the Rampant Rabbit has been the biggest-selling female sex toy in the world. At the time, men felt pretty threatened by a toy that was always up and on, but they soon realised that vibrators can't cuddle and they can't mow the lawn either.

Similarly, your husband will soon see that his Fleshlight may serve a purpose, but it won't serve him dinner and, between you and me, cleaning them out afterwards is a nightmare. So it is only a matter of time before his artificial vagina ends up out in the garage gathering dust with the breadmaker, the fondue set and the rowing machine.

Since my wife left me 8 years ago I have found myself watching more and more sexually explicit material on TV and the internet. This invariably leads to masturbation and emptiness. Sex now dominates my life unbearably. I would like a new relationship but I am in my mid-fifties and feel I lack the necessary social skills.

Yours sounds like a very sad, lonely and joyless existence. In shutting yourself off from reality, you seem to have imprisoned yourself in a nightmare and unless you can find a way to unlock the emotions behind your self-imposed isolation you face a spiralling descent into ever-increasing unhappiness.

Though the obvious trigger for your shrinking world would appear to be the end of your marriage, I don't believe that it is entirely responsible. You see, healing takes time, but it doesn't generally take eight years. People who have been scared or hurt often retreat into themselves in the aftermath of a major upset.

They try to protect themselves by shutting down and cutting themselves off from their feelings. They develop a kind of numbness, both physical and emotional, which forms a blanket over them until they grow stronger and feel ready to face society again. But they do eventually feel ready to do that. You, on the other hand, remain stuck in a darkened room staring at a screen with your life frozen in your hand.

That you have hidden yourself away for so long constitutes avoidance rather than upset. Staying at home and losing yourself in porn has become a means of preventing exposure to anything that might awaken feelings of unhappiness.

You say that you would like a new relationship, but like all people with avoidance issues you are afraid of being rejected, so you don't even try. You presume the worst and see others as potentially critical or uninterested without daring to test your core beliefs. And because you cannot tolerate your fears and feelings, you try to wipe them out instead. Some avoiders use drink or drugs or binge-eating. Others, like you, use sex.

Though the means are different, the end is the same. And although you probably don't even realize it, at this point your dependency on masturbation is both physiological and psychological. In the brain, pleasure and happiness are thought to depend on the levels of the chemicals serotonin, dopamine and noradrenaline (norepinephrine). In fact, most antidepressant pills work on stimulating the natural production of these chemicals.

Orgasm triggers the release of these feel-good chemicals and over the past eight years it would appear that this natural antidepressant has become the only 'relief' available to you. However, as with any drug, dosage gradually has to be increased to maintain efficacy.

The images that excited you in the past are no longer sufficient to jolt your depressed and desensitized brain into action and you have had to expose yourself to more and more explicit material to achieve the same levels of arousal. And because you don't have any friends, and you have lost your sense of perspective, and the internet is convenient, and completely anonymous, there is nothing to stop you sinking deeper and deeper into your dependency.

Without wishing to sound harsh, unless you are willing to help yourself the prognosis is grim. There is no point in my telling you to get yourself down to the social club or to try internet dating because if you want the quality of your life to improve, what you really need is psychiatry or cognitive therapy and, possibly, a course of antidepressants.

Make an appointment with your GP to discuss your

situation. He or she will decide if medication is appropriate and refer you to a counsellor.

You should also look at the Sex Addicts Anonymous website and try to find a local recovery group. Realizing that others share your problem can be very cathartic.

3.

Oedipus, cougars & getting back in the saddle

I'm a man in his 30s and I find I'm increasingly attracted to women twice my age or older. Is this an 'Oedipus complex' and do I need to seek help?

Are you attracted to 60+ women purely because they are over 60? Or have you become involved in a succession of relationships with women who just happen to be a lot older than you? If the answer to the first question is yes, then you could probably do with a little help. The psychoanalyst's view is that an Oedipus complex is not abnormal but, if you feel that what's happening is not natural, then a consultation with a therapist might help you to see whether this behaviour is something that you need to modify or accept.

If your attraction to elderly women is sexually compulsive, you might be classified as a gerontophile. Although this paraphilia is supposed to be very rare, if you type the words 'granny' and 'sex' into Google it brings up thousands of pages with self-explanatory titles such as Senior Sizzle or Hot Grannies. The abundance of explicit internet material catering to what must constitute 'niche' sexual behaviour suggests that you, and Jason from *Little Britain*, are not the only men in the country who get off on 'mature' women.

If your interest in older women is less a problem of sexual compulsion, and more a question of genuine interest, then you are part of a growing trend. The number of older women having relationships with younger men has increased dramatically in the past ten years. At this point all journalists writing on this subject are obliged to wheel out the actors Demi Moore and Ashton Kutcher as an example of how older women/younger men relationships are thriving. But, the thing is, Moore and Kutcher are separated only by 15 years and, let's face it, she hasn't got to 44 looking like she does without a little assistance.

Thanks to cosmetic surgery, medical science, better nutrition and a gym on every corner, older women look better and live longer than ever before. And, as divorce releases increasing numbers of middle-aged women back into the dating market, younger men have cottoned on to the fact that sex with a woman who is solvent, sorted and about to send her kids to college has enormous advantages. For postmenopausal single women, a relationship with a younger man can be liberating. And since nothing is ever certain, and things can go tits-up whether you choose a partner who is 32 or 62, these women are often happy to team up with a toy-boy regardless of how long the relationship lasts.

That said, 30 years is an enormous physical, mental and cultural gap for any couple to bridge. Dating someone who is frequently mistaken for your Nan might hold some erotic allure for a time, but the day-to-day reality of a relationship with someone who keeps her teeth in a glass is a little more complicated.

Vast age gaps mean vast differences. Perhaps the best example of how a relationship between an older woman and a younger man pans out in the long term is the partnership between Betty Dodson, in her seventies, and Eric Wilkinson, in his late twenties. Dodson has been one of America's leading sex educators for the past 30 years. She's been with Wilkinson for several years and they clearly have great sex, but aren't monogamous. Wilkinson has three other ongoing sexual relationships because, to quote Dodson: 'I'm feeling my years. I still love sex, but I can't f**k around the clock like I used to.'

I've been married for 20 years but my husband no longer has sex with me. A friend suggested that I hire a male escort and I'm tempted. Any advice?

Although the internet is awash with escort agencies professing to offer women absolutely anything they want – for a price – it would probably be more rewarding, and certainly less expensive, to try to get a rise out of that husband of yours.

I say this because, on your behalf, I have spent three hours trawling the net for male escorts and it was an incredibly depressing experience. Though the idea of 'dial a man' is cute in theory, in practice most of the agencies offering male escorts find it difficult to recruit men who want to do the job. Female prostitutes can fake arousal, but men can't fake an erection so there are more 'male escorts wanted' ads than there are agencies offering men.

None of the sites that I found offered photo galleries of their gents, but I had a little more luck with individual males advertising themselves as escorts. Some of these men also declined to provide images, but others such as, let's call him Mr X, appear in a range of looks, well, two to be exact: 'businessman' and... could that be 'rambler'? Mr X describes himself as an 'independent professional male escort' who is also a sports coach with two degrees. He is easy-going, a great listener, has a keen sense of humour, natch, and enjoys good food, wine and conversation. In his blurb he asks whether

'you would like to relax with some soothing aromatherapy?'
Or perhaps you might have 'some issues or problems that
you would like to discuss?' He doesn't say anything about
the size of his penis or how many positions he can get in to,
but there is a detailed price list which reveals that the bland
nearly bald male escort in the cheap suit is available 'for any
occasion' and can be yours for only £150 an hour.

And what do you get for that? In theory, you get 'no-strings
sex' with guaranteed discretion. An escort won't jeopardize
your marriage because the relationship is a purely financial
transaction. However, though you may try to rationalize it, in
reality it is a far more complicated exchange. I can't begin
to consider the mix of need and confusion that would drive
a man to sell himself for sex, but I can tell you that women
find it difficult to divorce sex from emotion. Although
attention bought from another man might, temporarily,
make you feel more sexual, and the clandestine nature of
your meetings would probably exhilarate you, betraying
your husband would almost certainly leave you feeling guilty.
And fear of being found out will make you feel anxious and
probably ashamed.

You think you would be satisfied by sex alone, but having
sex with someone who knows little and cares less about you,
is generally not a self-affirming experience. You are clearly
miserable in your marriage, but before you shell out for
sex with a stranger, it's worth giving your husband one
more chance.

The longer a couple avoid sex, the harder it is to restore
in the relationship. Sex therapy might help and he might
benefit from a course of Viagra to boost his confidence. If he
is suffering from any kind of erectile dysfunction, he needs
to see a doctor as it may indicate an underlying illness.

It's not going to be easy, but paying for sex is not the
solution because you will continue to share a bed with the
problem every night.

Since my marriage ended ten years ago I haven't had sex. I am a woman in my late fifties and the thought of it has now become terrifyingly remote. I had a very fulfilling sex life within my marriage. Should I resign myself to never having sex again, or should I be trying to do something about this?

Unless you are entertaining the idea of paying for sex, you can't really view it in isolation. People generally have to go to the trouble of having a relationship before they can 'have sex' and from what you say, you haven't had one of those since your marriage ended. Unfortunately, since there are roughly 5,000 women to every 3,000 men in your age bracket, you have your work cut out for you, but if you are prepared to be proactive there is every chance that you will find a partner.

Assuming that you've classified all the men in your existing social circle as either spoken for or unspeakable, the first thing you need to do is to broaden your horizons. I don't know how sociable you are, or what you are interested in doing, but if you are looking for a man, dating agencies are the obvious place to start.

Many agencies won't take women over 40 because they can't find any older men to match them with. Men tend to date downwards and given the choice between a 30-year-old and a 50-year-old, well, it's a no-brainer for the male ego, isn't it? If you have access to the internet you may have more luck with online introduction agencies. Saga has a chatroom or you could try Grapevine Social. A Google search of 'dating for older people' will bring up a whole lot more.

Personal ads might be an option, too. I know several people who have found partners this way. Placing an ad is more successful than responding to one because you can be specific about what you want and don't want. Make sure to word the ad carefully. In the personals, lots of phrases have double meanings ie; fun loving = sex mad; young at heart = 75+; young looking = 45+. Ageism is rife, so imply your own age but specify the precise age group that you are interested in meeting.

Choose a newspaper or magazine that reflects your values and interests and never reveal your phone number. If you get 15 replies, try to meet at least half of them. Choose a public place, tell a friend where you will be, take a mobile and, if you do get it on, use a condom.

Learning a new skill or taking up a hobby often leads to new friendships. You can take adult education classes in virtually anything and most institutions will allow you to sit in on one for free before you decide to join. This lets you check out suitable talent before you make a commitment. Dance classes are popular but there are usually more women than men. Bridge classes tend to be completely overrun with menopausal women, but cookery classes attract lots of divorced men learning how to boil an egg for the first time. Wine-tasting classes are always popular and no one ever spits out the wine.

Singles holidays can be great, but always check the age and ratio of men to women in the group. I went on a walking holiday with Exodus travel and there were 12 men and two women in my group. That's the kind of healthy ratio you are looking for. Solo Travel Online provides info on travel options for single people but your best bet is probably Saga holidays, which specializes in holidays for the over-50s. Let's hope they live up to their nickname – sexually active geriatrics abroad.

Since my wife walked out on our ten-year marriage three years ago, I have completely lost any desire to have sex, even though I have been dating some very attractive women. I am

in my early forties and am healthy and fit. Will I ever regain my sexual drive?

Well, I really do hope so, because nice, genuinely single chaps of 42 are a rare breed. Every dating agency in the country has a glut of attractive fortysomething divorcees with highlights on their books, and a complete dearth of middle-aged men to send them out on dates with.

So, if you can find your mojo, you will be as spoilt for choice as a kid in a candy store with a credit card. I realize that losing your wife, your confidence and your sex drive absolutely sucks but, unless you get rid of the nasty aftertaste that your marriage has left in your mouth, you won't regain your sexual appetite.

Being dumped is awful and, arguably, women have an easier time of it than men. We are allowed to blub our feelings out while we bore our sorority senseless, raking over every detail until we are sick of the sound of our own voices. But men don't have that opportunity. Because society says that 'big boys don't cry', the injured male must head off into the emotional badlands to lick his wounds alone. Then he digs a great big grave, buries all his feelings in it and comes back to town to get on with his life. He pretends that being dumped didn't hurt and that he didn't feel humiliated. He pretends that he can function socially and enjoy dating attractive women and that rage, abandonment, injustice, hurt, fear don't haunt him from their shallow grave. But of course they do.

So, although you are posing as a guy who is 'getting on with his life', I suspect that you and your life aren't getting on at all. Your lack of desire is a discomforting symptom but the real sickness is simply that you are still so bloody angry with your ex. It's not unusual. Anyone who has been dumped will be familiar with the relentless, obsessive mullings and surges of fury that take an all-consuming hold of mind and body. And anger is such a powerful physiological response that it is hard to combat rationally.

Anger is adrenalin-powered and this puts your body into a state of red alert, diverting blood flow away from extremities – such as fingers, toes and genitals – straight to the heart, lungs and muscles. Oh, and because an erection is the last thing you need before you thump someone, the blood vessels in your penis contract, rendering a hard-on impossible.

No matter how intellectual an approach you adopt to anger, or how much dust is supposed to have settled, if you don't diffuse your emotional bombs, unexpected triggers will continue to set them off for years. The stress of tiptoeing around volatile gelignite is a full-time job and if you are not careful it can become an excuse for not dealing with anything. Not processing your anger means that you are too traumatized to have a libido, which means you protect yourself from what you are most afraid of. Not wanting to have sex stops you forming a sexual relationship with a woman and, as such, negates the possibility of you getting hurt. Or laughed at. Or humiliated. Or compromised. Or rejected.

A GP would probably suggest a course of Viagra or Levitra, but this would be offering a physical fix to a mental problem. Though 'therapy' always sounds a bit ominous, I think a course of either sexual or cognitive therapy would help you enormously. Once you can see the link between your low sex drive, your self-esteem and your relationship history, you will be able to own your feelings, diffuse your bomb and get yourself back to the candy store where a thousand sweeties await you. Bonne chance.

I'm 39 and six months ago my husband and I divorced after 15 years of marriage. I have not been out with anyone except him since my early twenties but a while ago I joined

a dating website to meet new men. I met one I liked almost immediately and, after several dates, we went away for the weekend and had sex. I was very upset the following week when I found out that he was seeing several other women and that he didn't consider us 'exclusive'. I moved on and met another man and a similar thing happened. I am by no means ready to settle down again but I don't want to be part of a harem, as much for my teenage daughter's sake as mine. Is this the way dating works now?

Dating has always worked in this way. You meet someone new and you hang out together. You decide whether you are compatible – socially, emotionally, domestically, financially, spiritually – and somewhere along the way you test out your sexual compatibility, too. If everything clicks, the connection tends automatically to become exclusive because you both want to spend all your free time together, but making that commitment necessitates the shedding of various other halfs or admirers. Though 48 per cent of the adult population in the UK is now single, almost no one is completely up for grabs when you first meet them. Lurking somewhere there is always a friend with benefits, an ex who is still occasionally up for it, a long-term relationship that is grinding to a painful conclusion or, in the case of your last two relationships, an internet selection box that is begging to be sampled.

That the two men you dated were both seeing other women is not such a surprise. Internet daters have a tendency to go a bit wild in the aisles, even if it is only to feel that they are getting their money's worth, but most of them are only shopping for the right person and when they find him or her they head to the checkout. Because it can be such a rollercoaster, internet dating works best when it is used as a way of making new friends. Basically, the bigger your social circle and the more people you know, the more likely you are to find a solid relationship, but to get to that point you need to be actively open to opportunities. I get the feeling that you might not be emotionally ready for that yet.

This is a difficult time for you and although you probably can't see it, it is your own personal history that has sabotaged these two fledgeling relationships. Though you say that you don't want to settle down, your dating strategy seems entirely at odds with that statement. One egg, one basket and a lorryload of expectation … it's the behaviour of someone who is desperately searching for another long-term relationship. It's understandable. You are caring for your daughter, and it feels as if no one is caring for you, but no boyfriend can fill the divorce-shaped hole in your life.

In situations such as yours, a man seems the obvious solution, but women in the middle of an emotional crisis can have flawed judgment when it comes to rebound relationships. Occasionally, the fear of making a mistake prevents a woman who has been hurt taking what she perceives to be a risk, but more often the fear of being alone for ever makes a vulnerable woman mistake interest or even exploitation for passion and commitment. Studies by the psychologist Arthur Aron of the State University of New York indicate that stress hormones can distort romantic perception. As a result, anxious people tend to misinterpret physical cues and feelings – notably fear and thrill – for the sensation of falling in love.

With a teenage daughter to think about, it is a good idea to challenge your preconceptions about what it is that you are hoping to achieve from dating. Companionship and regular sex may be all that you want and need until your daughter is more independent. And don't forget to use a condom. Between 2002 and 2006 there was a 50 per cent rise in chlamydia and a 139 per cent rise in syphilis in men and women aged 45 to 65 in the UK.

4.

Going down
& the *quid pro quo*

Though my 29-year-old girlfriend easily has orgasms from
oral sex, she has never had an orgasm from penetrative sex.
She seems happy, but it leaves me feeling dissatisfied. She
wants to get married soon but I am worried that we may be
incompatible and that there could be someone better for both
of us. Is this something that can be overcome?

Female orgasm is incredibly elusive. Although most women
can climax perfectly well by themselves, partner sex is more
complicated. In the most comprehensive sex survey yet
carried out in the US, 61 per cent of women reported always
or usually experiencing an orgasm through masturbation,
but only 29 per cent reported always having an orgasm
during sex with a partner. This is mainly explained by the
fact that the clitoris, the most sexually sensitive part of the
female body, is located several centimetres away from the
vaginal opening.

   That biological anomaly could be overcome quite easily
if lack of communication were not also such a problem.
Women (young women in particular) rarely feel confident
enough to make sexual demands on a new partner and,
because porn movies have successfully propagated the myth

that vigorous thrusting is all it takes to make a woman climax, consecutive partners fail to provide meaningful clitoral stimulation and are left thinking that there is something wrong with them rather than something wrong with the kind of sex they are having.

As women mature, they develop a better understanding of their own responses and some realize that they can climax much more easily through oral sex. Most will have tried to convert the arousal they experience during oral into penetrative sex, only to discover that the physical transition kills the build-up of sensation. Unwilling to delay their partner, they eventually settle for guaranteed non-penetrative orgasm over an uncertain penetrative one.

It's not an unreasonable solution. An orgasm is an orgasm is an orgasm, and I'm sure your girlfriend doesn't care how she gets there, but she would be devastated if she knew how it was affecting you.

If you can find a way to get this out in the open, there are several practical techniques that could help you resolve the issue. First, when you have sex, begin switching between oral and manual stimulation to get your girlfriend accustomed to the sensation transition. You can then progress to penetration. My advice to her would be to concentrate on the pleasurable feelings. Continuity is vital – if you keep changing positions she will lose focus, so be patient and persevere. Also she should try going on top, which will allow her to control the pace. You may also want to try the 'coital alignment technique'. It is a revised missionary position that tilts the pelvis forward. It has been 'designed' to improve a woman's chance of experiencing orgasm during intercourse.

I am a 25-year-old girl and I've just met a wonderful man. I would like to give my boyfriend a proper blow job but whenever I try I just find myself choking. I know he likes it and

I want to give him pleasure but it feels so unnatural. Have you any tips for me?

Giving a blow job feels unnatural because it is unnatural. Bar a few well-trained, hollow-necked porn stars, few women are physically equipped to cope with an erect penis hitting the back of their throat because of the gag reflex, which has put many a woman off giving blow jobs for life.

Fortunately, help is at hand. I've had a word with a couple of technical experts and they have suggested the following tips. First, practise on a banana. It may sound a little bit like a schoolgirl prank, but unlike French kissing your arm, simulating oral sex with a piece of fruit can help you to control that choking feeling. It is all to do with managing your breathing correctly, apparently. If you exhale while going down to the base of the penis and inhale while going up, you learn to control the reflex and should eventually be able to take 10–15 cm (4–6 in) of banana at a time.

When you are ready to transfer your skills to your boyfriend, make sure you position yourself on top. This allows you to control the depth and frequency of penetration and - if you need a breather - you can stop whenever you want to.

If, on the other hand, you allow the man to be in control, try to keep one or two hands pressed against the base of his penis or his stomach so that you can push him away if you need to. My experts also suggest that you should wrap your thumb and forefinger around the base: this will make him feel like you are going all the way down – even though you are only doing the head.

The head of the penis contains 6,000 nerve endings so any kind of licking and sucking feels good. However, the most sensitive area tends to be the frenulum, the Y-shaped ridge at the back of the head, so concentrate some attention there. Don't be too timid and when you feel that he is enjoying a particular stroke or rhythm, don't change it, keep going.

If you want to increase the slip and slide, you could try using an oral lubricant. They come in a range of flavours: strawberry, chocolate, or even banana to remind you of your practice sessions. Alternatively, try sipping a little hot tea so that your mouth is hot when you go down on him and if you want to blow his mind, try filling your mouth with ice cubes or even peppermints before taking him on.

According to the experts 'if you can attend to the top 7 cm (3 in) of your boyfriend's penis with sensitivity and a degree of authority he will be more than satisfied.' And if your relationship is reciprocal and democratic I expect you will be too.

My husband of 30 years has become impotent. Viagra did nothing but give him a headache but we tried cunnilingus for the first time recently and I liked it, however I worry that he gets no pleasure from it. With the kids gone I feel more sexual, but all he wants is a cuddle.

I assume that your husband is still exploring treatment options but, if he isn't, he ought to make an appointment to see his GP as soon as possible. Alternatively, he could visit a GUM clinic (for genitourinary medicine) which has a sex therapy unit attached.

There are about 2.3 million men in the UK suffering from erectile dysfunction and any disorder illness which affects that many people attracts a lot of pharmaceutical investment, so new products to treat erectile dysfunction appear on the market all the time.

Viagra may have given your husband a headache, but what about Cialis, Levitra, Uprima or Muse? In the majority of cases, erectile dysfunction is caused by illness but several of these treatments are suitable for men with diabetes or heart disease, so all is not lost for him.

But what about you? You've been married for 30 years and you have only just tried cunnilingus. Hmm. No one could accuse you of being too assertive, could they? Ten thousand nights in bed with your husband and he has gone down on you ... once? Assuming that fellatio hasn't been off the menu, or penetration, I can't understand why you've never just pushed his head between your thighs and told him to get on with it. But I guess your fear that he might not enjoy it much goes back a long way.

Eliminating such a significant source of sexual pleasure from your love life has to involve a degree of complicity between both partners. You may have sensed a certain hesitation in the past and your instinct was probably right. Lots of men and women seem to be intimidated by giving and receiving oral sex. Suffice to say that most reasons for avoiding it can be overcome by a nice hot bath and a couple of glasses of chardonnay. And it is worth overcoming them because although cunnilingus is a bit of a mouthful to pronounce, it is consistently voted the 'most satisfying sex act' by women around the world. In a recent survey by NetDoctor, an independent health website, 51 per cent of women in the UK voted it their outright favourite form of sex. That figure would probably be higher if the 40 per cent of women who said they weren't getting enough got a bit more.

Although sex is portrayed in the media as some sort of enormous sensual smorgasbord, for most people '1,000 ways to orgasm' generally boils down to a meat-and-two-veg combination of manual, oral and penetrative. But even within the confines of this fairly limited menu, politeness, reticence and fear can make people compromise their sexual diet even further, mainly because they are too shy to tell their partner that they would like to try something different. How weird is that? If a couple are intimate enough to get naked, have sex, have kids even, it beats me how they can be too embarrassed to tell each other what kind of sex they enjoy. But it happens all the time.

Your husband would obviously prefer to have an erection but, if you explain to him how much you like cunnilingus, as a sensible man suffering from impotence, he will consider the fact that he can still bring you to orgasm orally to be a pretty good consolation prize.

In your current situation, cunnilingus offers you a whole new and exciting form of sexual pleasure, while simultaneously alleviating him from any pressure to perform penetratively. That's good for you. And good for him. So stop worrying and make the most of it.

I often have oral sex with my husband but we've heard that there is a link to throat cancer. We both had several partners before we met; am I at risk?

Honestly, just about everything that goes in to your mouth gives you cancer these days. It's typical, isn't it? Just when men are finally come to terms with the fact that 'going down' is a reciprocal sex act, along comes a throat cancer expert with news that oral sex gives you more than the big O.

Yup, the gentle arts of cunnilingus and fellatio are now officially life-threatening because Maura Gillison, MD, PhD, of the Johns Hopkins Bloomberg School of Public Health in Maryland, has established a direct link between oral sex and mouth and throat cancer.

All risk is relative and all scientific research is funded, but if you want specifics the study indicates that your personal risk depends on how many men you mean by 'several'. Dr Gillison says the risk of throat or mouth cancer is almost nine times higher for people who have had oral sex with more than six partners but, and this is the important bit, only because a greater number of sexual partners increases your chances of exposure to the human papilloma virus (HPV).

The majority of sexually active women will come into contact with higher risk HPV types at some time in their life, but HPV testing is not routinely available on the NHS and a private test is expensive, largely because most women get rid of the infection without even knowing it was there. According to Dr Gillison, the overwhelming majority of people with an oral HPV infection are unlikely to get throat or mouth cancer, but having said that, 50 years ago mouth cancer was five times more common in men than it was in women and now it is only twice as common in men.

While HPV has been implicated in the development of cervical cancer for years, Dr Gillison's study is important because it shows that HPV can also be transmited orally. It makes sense. The warm wet cells of the genitals provide a perfect breeding ground for any virus and, unsurprisingly, the cells in the mouth offer the same conditions. As a result, Dr Gillison can not even rule out the possibility that HPV can also be transmitted by kissing.

Her research is timely because two pharmaceutical giants are battling it out to corner the market with an HPV vaccine. GlaxoSmithKline is promoting Cervarix, an injection that targets two strains of the human papilloma virus. It is suggesting that if every one of the 376,385 12-year-old girls in the UK was vaccinated against the virus it would bring the death rate from cervical cancer down from 1,000 to 262 a year and the number of cases would apparently drop from 2,841 to 682 a year. The fact that this would simultaneously create an enormous cash cow for GlaxoSmithKline is obviously an incidental bonus, but the fact that this proposition is being taken seriously in the US explains why HPV is getting so much attention.

GlaxoSmithKline's rival is Gardasil, a vaccine that has

been developed by the company Sanofi Pasteur. It already has approval from the Food and Drug Administration and a European licence, and apparently provides protection from 85 per cent of HPV strains. It also has Dr Gillison on board to determine its potential in curbing oral cancers. Funny, that.

5.

Orgasms, inequities & Oscar–winning performances

I have read in magazines about G-spot orgasms and clitoral orgasms. What is the difference? And do all women have a G-spot?

Magazines are not a great source of sexual enlightenment for young women because they discuss the acquisition of clitoral and G-spot orgasms as if the process were an exact science. It is not. Female sexual function is so complicated that scientists cannot even agree on tangible stuff such as anatomical structure. The full extent of the clitoris was discovered only in 1997 when the Australian urologist Helen O'Connor, carried out post-mortem research on the sexual organs of ten women using 3-D photography.

She discovered that far from being the tiny hooded bean visible at the top of the labia, the 'body' of the clitoris is a large internal structure comprising two arms up to 9 cm (3½ in) long that flare backwards into the body. And despite the fact that it has had acres of press coverage, the existence of the G-spot has never been proved. Although some women experience increased sensation inside the vagina, scientists are not sure whether this is due to nerves, pressure on the urethra or impact on the internal extension of the clitoris.

There certainly doesn't seem to be a unique G-spot structure. In 1997, a review of all the available research on the subject was carried out by Dr Terence Hines of the Department of Psychology at Pace University, in New York. He failed to find any evidence to substantiate its existence. Indeed, Dr Hines declared the G-spot to be a 'sort of gynaecological UFO: much searched for, much discussed but unverified by objective means'.

It is hard to believe that any aspect of human anatomy could remain a mystery to scientists who have managed to clone sheep and graft human ears on to mice, but then female sexual function has never exactly been a scientific priority. This lack of information has led to much confusion and left many women feeling 'less than' because they don't appear to have a piece of anatomy that might not exist.

There are no universal truths about female orgasm because every woman is different, but in general, most women can achieve orgasm if they have enough clitoral stimulation and most can orgasm during penetrative sex if they have had enough clitoral stimulation beforehand.

However, few women can have a penetrative orgasm without any direct clitoral stimulation and although many women experience sensitivity and can orgasm, if the area known as the G-spot is stimulated, lots of women don't feel anything there at all.

There is really only one way to make your mind up on this issue and, fortunately, you don't need anyone to help you. To experience clitoral orgasm, just find your clitoris (8,000 nerve endings, you can't miss it), lubricate your finger and rub until you feel all fizzy and start juicing an internal lemon.

To find your G-spot, lie down on your bed, knees bent, feet flat with a small pillow under your bum. Insert your lubricated middle finger about 5 cm (2 in) into your vagina and press towards your navel. When you hit the right spot, pump firmly and it should start to feel nice. The sensation is less fizzy and more juicy. If you use the thumb of your other hand to gently stimulate your clitoris at the same time you should feel some very intense sensations. You may reach orgasm and even ejaculate. If you don't, don't worry about it.

Success is a journey, not a destination.

My partner experiences an extra shower of fluid which he finds most stimulating sexually when I orgasm. He's never come across anything like this before so he says. Am I one of the lucky few women who possess the pleasure treasure of female ejaculation? Release me from my curiosity.

Female ejaculation is not a common sexual phenomenon so it is unsurprising that your boyfriend has never encountered it before. The experience you describe was first documented by Dr Ernest Gräfenberg in 1950, though no one paid the concept much attention until Drs Beverly Whipple and John Perry packaged female ejaculation as the ultimate orgasm in 1981. Their book, *The G Spot*, promoted the theory that G-spot stimulation led to a kind of 'supergasm' which made women spurt a liquid which was comparable to male prostatic fluid.

Naturally, the idea caused a stir in the media and the ejaculatory orgasm was added to the ever increasing shopping list of 'must have' sexual experiences (which already included the clitoral orgasm, the vaginal orgasm, the multiple orgasm, the simultaneous orgasm and the G-spot orgasm).

The ejaculatory orgasm, however, proved to be so elusive that, unusually, men and women began to query the theory. Whipple and Perry stood their ground. They organized demonstrations in front of doctors – on stage and even live on radio – and eventually proved beyond reasonable doubt that a small percentage of women could spurt fluid like a man when they reached orgasm. But when tests on the composition of the ejaculate revealed traces of urea and creatinine, the primary components of urine, there then followed a great debate as to whether the emissions, which spurted from the urethra as opposed to the vulva, were to do with orgasm (yessss), or urination (yeuch).

Over two decades later, no one has managed to confirm female ejaculation as anything other than a spurt of urine caused by a brief relaxation of the bladder muscles after intense G-spot stimulation and orgasm.

Given that withholding the elimination of urine and faeces is one of our earliest personal responsibilities, few women care to think that their sexual excitement leads to such a loss of control and, as such, statistics suggest that the 'pleasure treasure' you describe affects fewer than 10 per cent of us.

Of that 10 per cent, the confident (like you) consider themselves to be members of an elite sexual club, while the insecure consider incontinence pants. If you didn't already know these facts, I hope that the reinterpretation of your 'lucky shower' as involuntary urination won't negatively affect your perception of an experience that seems to give you and your partner so much pleasure.

It is worth remembering that all sex is based on swapping bodily fluids, even urine, so the debate as to whether female ejaculatory fluid is urine or something comparable to male prostatic fluid is fairly irrelevant.

Most people tend to draw the line at sexual activities that involve human waste on grounds of hygiene, but although scatology is an extreme taste, urine doesn't really deserve the bad press it gets. Its composition is 95 per cent water and, since it is not an effective transmission fluid for infections or diseases, it is relatively safe. In fact, it has been ingested, injected and topically applied by millions of Indians as a medicinal cure for centuries.

Now, don't get me wrong. I'm not advocating golden showers or urine therapy. I'm merely pointing out that our reluctance to explore a certain bodily fluid is based on fears of infection which are actually unjustified.

It's also worth bearing in mind that had science managed to prove that female ejaculation was indeed a sign of superior orgasm, the world and its mother would be going to bed with plastic undersheets.

Ultimately, if your wet and wild orgasm makes you and your boyfriend happy, who cares whether the fluid you pass is wee or not?

Every time I orgasm with my partner, I wet myself a little. He finds this hilarious but I get embarrassed and have recently stopped climaxing. What can I do?

Make an appointment with your GP. Female incontinence is a much more common problem than anyone is prepared to admit. In a group of seven or eight middle-aged women, the chances are that one will have experienced a loss of bladder control. Incontinence can affect anyone at any age (500,000 UK children over the age of 5 can't control their bladders properly), but it is much more common during pregnancy, after childbirth and before menopause.

During pregnancy the growing baby squashes the bladder and urethra, sometimes pushing them out of position completely. Extra weight and pressure can also weaken the pelvic floor muscles and damage the bladder nerves. Vaginal delivery and episiotomy (the cut in the muscle that makes it easier for the baby to come out) can weaken bladder-control muscles and the bigger the baby the more likely it is that there'll be problems. Bladder control problems don't necessarily show up right after childbirth. Some women notice a weakness only in their forties and, as a woman approaches menopause and oestrogen levels decrease, the problem is likely to get worse. Oestrogen helps to keep the lining of the bladder and urethra plump and healthy and, as levels decline, the muscles that control the bladder weaken.

Because incontinence is embarrassing many women would rather disguise the problem with sanitary towels and vaginal deodorants than to seek help. It is often only when a woman is compromised in front of someone else, as you have been, that she is forced to address an issue that has been nibbling away at her quality of life for years. As is the case with so many 'embarrassing' personal issues, as soon as she tries to sort it out she realizes that she has been suffering in silence for no reason because the problem is as common as the solutions are varied.

Severe cases of incontinence may need surgery but whether the problem is major or minor, sufferers are always advised to strengthen their pelvic floor. Pelvic floor exercises involve tightening the muscles around your back passage, vagina and front passage. The sensation feels a bit like lifting a platform inside your pelvis and squeezing your muscles around it. You hold the 'lift and squeeze' for as long as you can and then rest for four seconds, making sure to breathe normally. You repeat the process ten times, three or four times a day, gradually increasing the time that you can hold each contraction. Women who are not sure they are working the right muscles may want to invest in a pelvic toner. The product is designed to combat incontinence and improve sexual satisfaction.

Improving pelvic tone can take months. In the meantime, remember to pee before you have sex and try not to get wound up about leaks. Sexual intercourse is synonymous with the emission of bodily fluids and urine is nothing to be afraid of. It's 95 per cent water. It doesn't leave a stain. And, dare I say it, for many couples a warm, wet, golden shower is one of the nicest ways to say I love you.

My new partner can clamp my penis during sex and at orgasm she has such strong spasms I'm worried that I'll get stuck inside. Is this possible?

Blimey. What a pelvic floor your woman must have. She definitely hasn't had four kids, I can tell you. And her climax must be off the Richter scale. Most women would give their right arm, well, possibly their appendix or tonsils, for that kind of vaginal control. But, unfortunately, there is only one way of becoming the Fatima Whitbread of sexual penetration and, like almost every other kind of self-improvement, it involves long-term commitment and a degree of effort.

The pelvic floor and all the other bits and pieces that make up a woman's internal genitalia are held in place by a sling of muscle called the pubococcygeus muscle and, like any other muscle, this can be strengthened through exercise. The correct way to do it was discovered in 1947 by Arnold Kegel, a Californian gynaecologist.

Kegel was trying to help people suffering from incontinence; however, his patients soon realized that the exercises helped them with more than just urinary control. A toned pelvic floor, as Kegel's patients discovered, also enhances orgasm immeasurably.

Kegel is famous for his pelvic workout but less well known as the inventor of the perineometer, a device that can measure the strength of a woman's pelvic floor. Though they are mostly used in a medical context now, in the early 1970s Betty Dodson, a feminist activist, ran orgasm workshops for women which involved participants taking turns with a condom-clad perineometer. She compared it to the strong men in the circus swinging a mallet to ring the bell and, when someone scored a perfect 100 squeezing the perineometer with her pubococcygeus muscle, Dodson rang a bicycle bell while the rest of the group applauded. Despite being in her seventies, Dodson is still hell-bent on raising female sexual consciousness. She has made her own contribution to the strength of the female pelvic floor in the form of Betty's Barbell, a stainless steel vaginal exerciser and pleasure device, which is, according to the website, 'sturdy enough to become a family heirloom.' Bless.

But I digress. What you really want to know is whether your penis could get stuck inside your extra-strong mate? Well, it might if you were a dog or a wolf. Male canids have a penis with a particularly bulbous head and during mating they can remain locked or tied inside the female for as long as 20 minutes after ejaculation. However, although the phenomenon you describe has an impressive Latin title, there is no evidence that *penis captivus* has ever occurred during human sexual intercourse.

The first report of it dates back to 1884 when *The Philadelphia Medical News* published an article on the subject, written by Egerton Yorrick Davis. But the article turned out to be a hoax perpetrated by Sir William Osler, a prominent Canadian doctor with a sense of humour.

A detumescent penis would slide out of even the tightest vagina and *penis captivus* is now widely believed to be an urban myth, so relax.

I am an attractive, self-assured 30-year-old woman. I have had several sexual partners and all my experiences have been pleasurable. However, I have never had an orgasm with a man. I am able to bring myself to a climax, alone, within minutes. So why can't I do this with someone else?

I can't deduce whether you have admitted the fact that you have not had an orgasm to any of your partners, but I suspect not. And this is probably your biggest mistake.

It means that every sexual encounter you have is coloured by your apprehensions and the fact that you've never had an orgasm with a man then becomes a self-fulfilling prophecy.

Being honest is fundamental to a good relationship and if you don't feel you can be open with a partner, you should question why you are having sex with him. That said, your situation is far from unusual. Only 75 per cent of men and 29 per cent of women always have orgasms with their partner. Those figures don't illustrate that men are selfish lovers. They merely demonstrate how little women know about their own bodies. When young girls discover orgasm it is often the result of an accidental realization that riding a horse or pulling a nightie between the thighs 'feels nice'. As they get older, many women then find that they can't move on from the methods they employed as children. The sensation gap between what they do to themselves (clitoral masturbation) and what happens in a sexual relationship (vaginal penetration) seems too big and the fear that 'orgasm won't happen' or 'there's something wrong' takes hold. A woman who can't express this to a partner then finds herself stuck.

Immobilized by her perceived inadequacy, no matter how much she wants to translate the sex she can have by herself into sex she can share with her partner, she can never relax enough to go over the edge. That's the bad news. The good news is that once you are prepared to be honest and your partner is prepared to be supportive, you are fully equipped to enjoy orgasm with your partner.

Your first step is to do what you do to yourself in front of him. Don't change your usual technique. Close your eyes, fantasize, and keep going until you climax. It may take longer than it does when you are alone but since you know that this technique works for you, persevere, because at this point the barrier is psychological rather than physical.

Once you can make yourself come in front him, the next step is to allow him to do it for you. This is where many women lose confidence and a lot of men lose patience, so before you start, it is important to secure his assurance that he will carry on stimulating you until you climax. Only then will you be able to relax enough to fully enjoy the experience.

You may find yourself putting up physical barriers if the sensations you experience are different from those you create for yourself, but try to suspend your disbelief. Help him out, give some guidance, close your eyes, concentrate on 'feeling' what is happening to you, and you can, I promise you, climax. (You may orgasm more quickly if your partner rubs a lubricated vibrator over your clitoris, but if you get used to the powerful sensation of the vibrator you may find more subtle stimulation is not strong enough).

As your confidence builds, you should be able to switch to penetrative sex and achieve orgasm with your partner inside you. It may take a while for you to get used to the change in sensation but you will considerably increase the chance of success if you are on top. In this position penetration is deeper and, more importantly, you can continue to stimulate the 8,000 nerve endings in your clitoris by rubbing yourself against his pelvis.

And the 6,000 nerve endings in his penis will be delighted by the result.

6.

Blindfolds, nipple clamps & swinging for beginners

I have been married for 20 years and our sex life has become a little flat. My wife has suggested that we try role play. Do you have any ideas?

Though the end result is always the same – getting naked and having sex – role play involves a greater degree of planning and preparation than the average domestic shag, so it automatically heightens sexual tension and anticipation.

Because it often hinges on the deliberate imbalance of erotic power, and in that sense overlaps with submission and domination, role play doesn't appeal to everyone. Some people feel threatened by anything other than straightforward sex. Others lack the imagination to get beyond the dodgy doctor's and nurse's outfit and feel their way into an emergency-room sex drama. They feel stupid, not sexy, and that's a real passion-killer.

It's difficult to know what impact role play will have on your sex life until you have tried it, but you have nothing to lose by giving it a whirl. The most common sexual scenarios involve a stereotypical relationship in which one character has authority and control over the other: doctor and patient; maid and employer; sex worker and client; teacher and student; or even owner and dog (basically any relationship in which one party might feasibly deserve being manhandled, told off or given a good hiding).

Costumes and props are essential and the more effort you put in to the way you look the more impact you will have. Most sex shops sell crotchless, topless, bottomless versions of the obvious favourites. You can pick up the Hail Mary or the Fireman's Lift at Ann Summers, but for a more convincing disguise you might consider visiting a medical, military, sports or school uniform supplier for the real thing. Props such as latex gloves and thermometers can be bought at pharmacies, while canes, cricket bats and hockey sticks can generally be found in second-hand shops or car-boot sales. A builders' merchants will be good for overalls, hard hats, tool belts; while more radical concepts, such as religious costumes, can be catered for by fancy-dress hire shops.

If you are going to invest a lot in your outfit then consider location, too. It's easier to keep up the illusion of being someone else in an environment appropriate to the scenario you are acting out (though you should obviously ensure that your actions won't cause offence, or get caught on CCTV and/or get you arrested). Going for a drive in the countryside and picking up your role-playing hitchhiker for an impromptu picnic combines the thrill of anonymous sex with the joys of the great outdoors. If you have keys to the office, going in at the weekend to play 'interview the new secretary' is popular.

Libraries are good fun, too. There is something about imposed silence that brings out the rebel in all of us. Picture yourself sitting across the room from a demure, bespectacled woman wearing a heavy tweed skirt with sensible lace-up shoes and blouse, reading Anaïs Nin. Visualize yourself watching other people watching her. You stare at her until, eventually, she makes eye contact. As you replace your book on the shelf you brush past her and whisper a suggestion

in her ear. She replies in French and silently begins to
pack her bag. Visualize other people watching you leave
the library together. You remain in character as you walk
home. Indoors, you remove her glasses, unpin her hair and
unbutton the impossibly thin fabric of her blouse. '*J'aime les
choufleurs, mon petit pois*,' she whispers (any old tripe sounds
sexy in French).

And then you get naked and have sex.

**My wife of 25 years and I are very excited about the prospect
of swinging. We have spoken to others and practise safe sex.
Any last minute advice?**

Personally, I'd rather gnaw my own kidney out than go
anywhere near communal coupling, but then, I've never
been good at sharing. Swinging scares me, but according
to the North American Swingers Club Association (whose
slogan is: 'For those who want more than just one bite'),
my reaction is normal. It says that swinging induces
apprehension in less adventurous types because 'our fear
that love is scarce encourages us to hoard love. But hoarding
love creates the very scarcity that was feared to begin with.'
No, I don't really understand that either.

Swinging originated in the States. It first hit the headlines
when high fatalities among an elite group of US Air Force
fighter pilots during the Second World War, led to an
unusual closeness between the widows, wives and pilots left
behind. By the late Fifties, the phenomenon had spread
from the bases to the suburbs and the media had coined the
term 'wife swapping'.

By the early Sixties, 'key parties' were the thing. Men
would put their keys in a bowl and women would select a set
at random and have sex with their owner, though, even the
dimmest wit realized that the Porsche key got picked out

quicker than the Ford pick-up. The emergence of swinging magazines and permanent clubs made it easier and more acceptable for sexually curious couples to find each other, and although it still has a terribly Seventies image (picture Bjorn from Abba, naked, in a faux-Greek living room, with nibbles and Asti Spumanti), swinging continues to attract new followers.

Though the North American Swingers Club Association has five million members, swinging isn't tolerated in the same way in the UK. There are numerous couples' clubs throughout the country but the police don't take kindly to them and swing-club owners have faced prosecution on the grounds of keeping a brothel and living off immoral earnings. The risk of police intervention makes it difficult for investors to raise capital and create decent clubs and, as a result, the British version of swinging tends to be a shabby, underground affair.

Swing protocol varies from person to person. Some swingers prefer not to be around when their partner is having sex with someone else (closed swinging); others insist on it (open swinging). Some will go only as far as heavy petting and switch back to their partner for any actual sex (soft swinging), and 10 per cent don't swing at all and simply watch. Safe sex is obviously a must, so clubs advise swingers to use money belts to store condoms, lube and any other accoutrements that they might need.

Dr Ted McIlvenna, the president of the Institute for Advanced Study of Human Sexuality, in San Francisco, who began studying swingers 12 years ago, says that, initially, it's nearly always the man in a couple who wants to try swinging, but it's the woman who wants to go back again and again. He suggests that men go to swinging clubs to get laid, but that women appreciate the sense of community, bless them.

The reality is probably more to do with the fact that most swing clubs already have their fair share of sex-mad fantasists, so when Mrs Shyboots finds herself unexpectedly in demand, she loves every minute of it. As such, if I have any advice for you, it is to make sure that you and your wife are confident that you will be able to cope with the unforeseen pressures to which you are about to expose your relationship.

I'm 40 and my husband of ten years has recently suggested that we try a threesome with another woman. He says he thinks that one of his colleagues from work would be keen. I'm not sure about this – is it a bad idea?

It's not a bad idea – it's a terrible idea. I don't want to rain on your candy floss, sweetie, but this is the real world not The Waltons. Let me explain something to you. Your husband of ten years doesn't just 'think' that one of his colleagues from work 'might' be keen. It's odds-on that he knows it for a fact because he has been shagging her for months.

Threesomes are not the kind of thing that male and female office colleagues discuss around the water-cooler. They whisper these fantasies to each other when they are post-coital, *a deux* – or possibly *a trois*, if Sharon from reception got really drunk with them the night before.

Females who get off on threesomes do exist, though there are not many of them and they don't generally work in offices. There's Abi Titmuss, of course, but I think it's fair to say that most heterosexual women prefer to have one-on-one sex with their man.

Males are different. They start fantasizing about threesomes when they emerge from the womb and see a nurse and a midwife gazing fondly at them. For a man, a threesome is the ultimate ego trip. Two women pleasuring him. Two women pleasuring each other to pleasure him. Him pleasuring two women. It is the stuff that dreams are made of – well, male dreams anyway – but most men are content to leave it at that. When a married man single-handedly sets up a threesome, without consulting his wife, he is disrespecting her.

Some men argue that it is a positive way of reviving a flagging sex life because it involves both partners, but that's rubbish. In the majority of cases a dominant partner forces the issue, knowing that the subservient partner will go along with it because she, or he, is intimidated, or absolutely terrified of losing the relationship.

I discussed this issue with a relationship counsellor who has a great deal of experience in this area. She has counselled numerous women who reluctantly involved themselves in threesomes, swinging or dogging situations to make their partner happy. Needless to say, it never worked. The initial relationships invariably split up and the women who then paired up with partners that they met through swinging condemned themselves to a life where swinging was not only accepted but expected.

No disrespect but, to be honest, most women with an intact bulls**t detector know all this stuff intuitively. If their husband raises the idea of a threesome, they smell a rat immediately. If he then goes on to suggest that he has already recruited a willing third party from his office, they smell a whole damn sewer.

Though I have no idea how you will choose to handle this situation, you could consider the following. Suggest that you are up for a threesome but want to experience the delights of two men rather than two women and see how he reacts.

Alternatively, sit him down at the kitchen table and ask him to explain, in as much detail as possible, what it is about the colleague who will be joining in that appeals to him. Ask him to describe her, whether she is sexy, how he knows that she will agree to it, whether he has already had sex with her and what he wants you to do with her.

Then, when you feel that you have all the relevant

information, you need, turn off the video camera that you have hidden behind the plant pot on the fridge. Take the tape and get it transferred to DVD, and send copies of it to one, or all, of the following people: a) the 'keen' colleague; b) his mum; c) your lawyer.

7.

Scarlett Johansson, spanking & getting tied up in knots

The only way I can get it up with my wife of 30 years is to think of a young girl: Scarlett Johansson is my favourite. Am I being unfaithful?

No. As someone once said, getting married for sex is like buying a 747 for the free peanuts. Thirty years of intercourse with a person who takes up a little more of the bed each year justifies the use of imagination, so don't beat yourself up about your Scarlett fantasy. What your wife doesn't know won't hurt her and, besides, when she closes her eyes and gets that look, you know, like she's concentrating, well, she probably is. On Johnny Depp.

Though fantasizing is viewed as acceptable during solo sex, it seems a bit irreverent during intercourse, so people tend to keep their thoughts to themselves. However, several researchers, from Alfred Kinsey onwards, have managed to quantify both the number of men who fantasize about sex (54 per cent) every day and how many times a day they do so (three to seven times). Until now, no one has bothered to analyse what people think about, but that's about to change.

A team of psychologists at the University of Leeds, led by Dr Mitch Waterman, have been conducting a study of male sexual fantasy (a female study will follow). Nothing is off limits – bestiality, rape, sadism – and Waterman hopes that anonymity and confidentiality will encourage men to share the entire spectrum of their sexual thoughts.

The team have collected 2,000 responses and are beginning to analyse the data. So far, their research suggests that the most common sexual fantasy in both heterosexual and homosexual men is 'sex with a loved partner'. What? I have to admit I laughed when Dr Waterman told me that. And, reassuringly, he laughed, too. He explains the result as 'having an element of socially desirable responding'. In other words, men can't even admit to themselves that they fantasize about someone else when they are having sex.

Dr Waterman is collecting his data from 'normal' guys as well as convicted sex offenders (apparently sex offenders have more sexual problems and find it difficult to use fantasy to masturbate to orgasm). At the moment he is looking at younger men (they fantasize more broadly) but he also plans to explore the 'nature of the changes that fantasies undergo as people age'.

The study makes a clear distinction between thinking about doing something and actually doing it. Dr Waterman cites the example of a wife who has fantasies about getting revenge on her ex-husband but would never actually act on them, and he suggests that the same is true of people's sexual fantasies. For example, previous research shows that about 35 per cent of men admit to fantasizing about forced sex, yet only a tiny percentage of deviant men actually act on that fantasy and rape someone.

Dr Waterman believes that it is guilt – the emotion that is nagging away at your conscience – that keeps the psyche in check. Guilt reins in fantasies and creates a vital boundary between 'thinking' and 'doing'. Therefore, since there is little danger of you actually having sex with Miss Johansson, you are not being unfaithful and there is no harm in your fantasy – as long as you remember to beat yourself up about it occasionally.

When I'm having sex with my husband I can orgasm only when imagining myself with a woman. I've never actually been attracted to another woman in real life, only the fantasy. Is this a problem? Should I tell him?

No, no, no. What is it with this obsessive need to 'share'? Yes, emotional honesty is fundamental to a solid relationship, but so, too, is autonomy. Your husband doesn't need to know every little thing that goes on in your head. If you tell him that you fantasize about having sex with another woman while he does his thing, you risk making him feel redundant, or threatened, or undermined. Suddenly you become accountable for something hypothetical. Your fantasy is not real, but the feelings that it stirs are.

Alternatively, your revelation might be a massive turn-on for him. If that happens, the fantasy stops being yours and starts being his, which poses other problems. For a start, it encourages reciprocity. Do you really want to give your husband permission to confess his fantasies about Angelina, or Brad, or both? And would a positive response from your husband leave you feeling anxious, or uneasy? If he was really keen, does it mean he is bored? Would you then find yourselves moving one step closer to an ad in the personals – 'Couple plus one for fun and games'? Sexual fantasy is a private opportunity to explore the sex you will never have with people who will never have you. It's escapism, a fast-forward to arousal, and the general consensus among therapists is that it is harmless as long as it doesn't become obsessive or put anyone at risk.

Why women, though? Well, in fantasy, there is no risk, no accountability and no consequences, so ideas that you might find fascinating and also repellent can be tested without fear. There are all sorts of theories about why this might be the case.

Evolutionary psychologists suggest that because sexual fantasies trigger arousal, they may play an important role in procreation. Freudian psychoanalysts, by contrast, speculate that fantasy is a form of wish fulfilment and a mechanism for overcoming memories of early traumatic experiences. Alfred Kinsey's research on human sexuality suggested, wrongly, that women confined their fantasies to the level of their own sexual experience.

In the 1970s, Nancy Friday's research into female sexual fantasy indicated that many young women felt so guilty about their fantasies that they couldn't allow themselves to think about consensual sex and fantasized about romanticized rape. Later, in her book *Women on Top*, Friday argued that having started a revolution for equality, women should complete it by freeing their sexual fantasies. Arguably, that has happened now. The prevalence of pornography has almost certainly filtered through into female fantasy, and since girl on girl is a staple of all X-rated fare, the chances are that your lesbian fantasy is simply a replication of a narrative that you have borrowed.

Fantasy is a particularly interesting aspect of human sexuality because it is a 'thought' rather than a 'deed', and therefore one of the more mysterious aspects of our nature. However, our understanding of the subject improved recently thanks to the psychoanalyst Brett Kahr. Kahr teamed up with Mori – the research company – and got nearly 20,000 people to tell him whether they fantasized and what they fantasized about. The results, which are published in his book *Sex and the Psyche*, suggest that 96 per cent of males and about 90 per cent of females have sexual fantasies. Kahr also discovered that because most people's sexual fantasies revolve around someone other than a current long-term partner, 95 per cent of people never share their fantasies with another person. I repeat: they NEVER share their fantasies with another person.

I found some porn that my husband had downloaded on our computer (I subsequently discovered that he had wanted me to find it) with a lot of images of dominant women and submissive men. He says that it is something that he is very drawn to. I am quite open-minded and excited by the idea, but I don't know where to start. Your advice would be appreciated.

The current celebration of leather and wet-look PVC, plus burgeoning bondage sections in every online sex store, are testimony to the fact that it has gone mainstream. From leopardskin blindfolds to snakeskin whips or Swarovski crystal handcuffs, fashionable restraint is a consumer-driven experience – and the imagery associated with it nearly always features an aesthetically bound woman, the assumption being that the male is dominant.

However, as you may soon find out, 'bondage lite' has very little in common with the experience that your husband is steering you towards. If you agree to allow your husband to explore his submissive side, you are, in effect, volunteering to take on the role of dominant partner in your physical relationship and you ought to be aware that this contract may permanently alter the sexual dynamic between you.

On a practical level, if your husband is physically restrained, he relinquishes all control and you are forced to become the pro-active sexual partner. That's quite a responsibility because, although the word submission implies passivity, most male submissives want to be actively taken in hand, which involves you making demands and meting out punishments when you may prefer to be watching Corrie.

On the plus side, male submissives don't confine their desire to serve to sex alone and they tend to be very handy with a hoover and a duster, too. Elise Sutton, a psychotherapist, explains that what submissive males are searching for is not merely an alternative form of sexuality, but a kind of 'loving female authority', which ultimately empowers women. And certainly, any women who take on the role of 'domme' seem to relish it.

However, before you make any promises to him, make sure that you are fully aware of what you might be letting yourself in for. The best books on the subject are *The Mistress Manual: The Good Girl's Guide to Female Dominance*, by Mistress Lorelei, *The Art of Sensual Female Dominance: A Guide for Women*, by Claudia Varrin, or *Screw the Roses, Send Me the Thorns: The Romance and Sexual Sorcery of Sadomasochism*, by Philip Miller and Molly Devon. You can also learn a lot from online forums.

As the dominant partner, you will be responsible for your husband's safety, so you will need to know what you are doing. Submission and domination come in a range of strengths – from fluffy handcuffs to masks that render the wearer deaf and blind – and it is only through experimentation that you and your husband will you find what works for you.

To test the water, you and your husband may want to try dressing up and visiting a fetish club. If you stick to larger commercial venues such as Torture Garden, you will be able to blend in and observe the theatre without worrying about participation.

My man and I have discussed my getting a clitoral piercing. He's very keen and says it would turn him on, but I'm not so sure. Would it make sex better for me?
No, no, no, no, no. Good God, woman, why would you

want to have a metal bolt rammed through the 8,000 most significant nerve endings in your anatomy? Are you mad? Have you seen all those pictures of scraggy, pierced and plucked chicken flesh on Tribalectic.com?

I know every one of the female colanders who post their personal experiences on that website enthuses about how sexually stimulating they find their clitoral piercing but, hey, some people find having cigarettes stubbed out on them while they are chained to a rack sexually stimulating too.

For a tiny number of women with large desensitized and protruding clitorises, piercing can supposedly help to restore sensitivity, but these women are in a small minority and, since you don't mention specific sexual difficulties, I doubt that this applies to you.

I know piercing is hip, but I really cannot see the point in irreparably jeopardizing the efficacy and well-being of your most precious sexual asset just so that you can wear an earring in it.

Any procedure that cuts through so many important nerves is seriously risky and, once the local anaesthetic wears off, seriously painful, too, so don't allow yourself to be manipulated into this just because it appeals to your boyfriend. In fact, if he is such a big fan of genital piercing, why don't you suggest that he tries it first; something like the 'amphallang', a piercing that involves drilling a hole horizontally through the head of the penis. There's a selection of photos of amphallangs in the Tribalectic picture gallery.

Though piercing websites give the impression that you can have yourself stapled top to toe if you fancy, clitoral piercing is actually so difficult that reputable practitioners often advise women to go for a clitoral hood or labia (vaginal lips) piercing instead. The clitoral hood can be pierced horizontally or vertically, depending on its shape and size, but the vertical option is, apparently, the easier, less painful, most stimulating, and fastest healing genital piercing.

A curved barbell or captive bead ring is inserted into the hood tissue just above the clitoris so it rests easily on the clitoris and, because the piercing runs parallel with your natural contours, there is little twisting or binding.

Personally, I still fail to see the attraction, possibly because I can't see how one can reconcile an interest in Agent Provocateur lacy knickers and snagtastic genital jewellery; possibly because I am just out of touch with the sexual delights of hole punching. Not that my opinion matters because the decision to have your clitoris pierced, or not, will probably be taken out of your hands. The size of the clitoris varies so much that the majority of women who present themselves for clitoral piercing are turned away because they are not anatomically suitable. Some women's clitorises are hidden too far under the clitoral hood to pierce and this is a problem because if the jewellery constricts and twists underneath the hood, the piercing can migrate, reject or scar. The clitoris must be at least 6 mm (¼ in) wide to hold a piercing safely without causing permanent nerve damage.

Piercing the clitoris can result in excessive bleeding, not to mention chronic irritation, pain and infection. Now would that make sex better for you? I don't think so.

8.

Rubber boots, Yogi Bear & Mum's lycra leggings

I have developed a fetish for black rubber, to the extent that I practically live in black wellies. How can I persuade my girlfriend to share my kink?

If your girlfriend realizes that your fondness for black wellies is nothing to do with puddles of mud – and she is still with you – you are off to a good start.

Frankly, most straight women would have shown you and your wellies the door the second they suspected that you were having an affair with them.

Getting off with your gumboots isn't exactly infidelity but to non-rubberists your fetish is threatening and bewildering. Threatening, because most people don't understand whether rubberists are turned on by the skin-tight material sprayed on to the curvaceous body of the page three model, or the curvaceous body of the model. Bewildering, because they can't figure out what latex has that they haven't.

There is consensus among rubberists who have non-rubberist partners that it is better to tell the truth about a fetish sooner rather than later. Needless to say, that's easier said than done. Most fetishists have harboured their secret for years and sharing it is such a terrifying prospect that many choose to hide their feelings rather than jeopardize their relationships.

However, in a long-term partnership, it becomes increasingly difficult to avoid arousing suspicion. Some, like you, introduce their fetish in acceptable forms (wellies) in the hope that it will create a tolerance to the more elaborate (full rubber body-suit with peephole headmask). This approach, however, nearly always goes belly-up because it is impossible to gauge a person's understanding of something as alien as a rubber fetish without some open discussion.

Rubberists who have confessed their secret to non-rubberist partners, and lived to tell the tale, recommend trying to divorce your individual fetish from the wider 'fetish scene'. Fair or not, fetishists are generally perceived as weird, and as people tend to lump fetishes together, your girlfriend will probably find it easier to accept it if you emphasize that your fetish is specifically confined to rubber.

In explaining this to her it will probably help if you attach feelings or senses to the material itself. One rubberist describes the sensation of touching the 'smooth elastic texture of vanilla-scented latex stretched tight over soft skin' as a 'sensitivity multiplier'. If your partner understands that it is the smell, the look, the feel of this material that amplifies your sexual feelings, she will feel less threatened by it.

If you want your girlfriend to try wearing rubber, bear in mind that most women have body-image issues and feel nervous about squeezing into a tight little anything. Reassure her that because rubber is thick and matte it holds things in place and when stretched tightly, creates dramatic visual contrasts, which emphasize every curve and contour.

To illustrate this you might show her the Breathless website – one of a number of companies that specialize in latex couture. They have an extensive range, from basic bikinis to floor-length fantasy gowns. They also stock popular labels such as House of Harlot and Velda Lauder.

If these amazing outfits don't appeal to her, you could always buy her wellies.

I have a masochistic kink. How can I persuade my straight-laced (though loving) wife that occasionally beating my bum with a hairbrush before, during, or sometimes instead of sex, is harmless fun rather than a disgusting perversion?

I have to admit that I'm curious as to how you managed to meet, marry and get a mortgage with your strait-laced wife without ever mentioning your 'masochistic kink'. It strikes me as odd that you could develop such an intimate relationship yet fail to share the fact that you have a penchant for being spanked on the bum. And I suspect that it will strike your wife as kind of odd, too.

Having a fetish is not a big deal as long as your partner digs it and no one gets hurt. But since your wife didn't vow to share her marital bed with a hairbrush, you ought to appreciate that the biggest hurdle you face won't be persuading her that spanking is fun but convincing her that your sex life to date has not been a total sham.

A hairbrush fetish doesn't constitute infidelity in a physical sense, but you haven't exactly been honest with her, have you? If she sees your 'kink' as undermining the connection between you, or her sexual significance to you, not only will there be no spanking, there will be no sex either. So tread carefully because you are, in effect, treading on her ego.

If you tell her the truth she will undoubtedly have questions. How long have you felt like this? Have you done it before? Where? With whom? Mason Pearson or Denman? One of her main concerns will be trying to establish the level of masochism attached to your 'kink'. Like piercing, spanking can be as 'aah' as a pearl earring or as 'ouch' as a Prince Albert, and right now you are the only one who can reassure her that what you want really is only harmless fun.

Since fetishes don't appear overnight she will probably conclude that this has been preying on your mind for some time. And as you don't appear to have had an outlet for your interest she will probably accuse you, rightly or wrongly, of indulging it online. This may be your undoing because the majority of spanking websites are a rather disturbing collection of images of red raw bottoms with whiplash marks, weeping wounds, welts and blisters. If your wife sees any of this, you will be using a comb until you go bald.

If you want to avoid the Spanish Inquisition (though you might actually get off on that), I suggest that, initially, you should dress up your rather specific fantasy as a general desire for more experimental sex.

Though relatively few people get into heavy fetish, most couples mess around with blindfolds and restraints (we're talking Rotary Club ties and nylon tights, not cuffs and manacles) at some stage. And if your wife is open to the suggestion of gentle bondage, theoretically you should then be able to introduce your hairbrush as a natural extension of this mild sub/dom behaviour.

By knitting it into a wider process of sexploration, your longing to be spanked won't stand out as a screaming fetish and that might make it more acceptable to her.

The fact that your wife is 'strait-laced' may actually work in your favour, too. Spanking is a form of sexual role play and people typically choose 'personalities' which are very opposite to their real character.

Your rather conservative wife might just come into her own as a mistress/dominatrix if you give her enough encouragement. And it will, of course, give her an opportunity to punish you for the fact that you have kept your 'dirty little secret' from her for so long.

In my native New York, I used to dress as Yogi Bear and have sex with like-minded women. Now I live in the UK and I've met a girl; should I tell her I'm a 'furry'?

Rubber? Fine. Leather? Of course. Polyester faux fur? Um, no. Blame the stiff upper lip but when it comes to fetishes, being tied up and spanked by a stoic in squeaky lace-up shoes is a much more British cup of tea.

We like our fetish to be restrained – suppression, inhibition, secrecy, pain, lying back and thinking of England without removing one's black ankle socks, that kind of thing. Not for us the flamboyant joviality of dressing up as teddy bears and making out like rabbits.

To the average British person, dressing up in furry animal outfits is something associated with theme parks, children's party entertainers and charity fundraisers. Running 26 miles on a hot summer's day dressed as a chicken is perfectly acceptable, but an erotic interest in Pudsey, the retinally challenged Children in Need teddy, is not in our cultural script. And when it comes to women, particularly doe-eyed college girls with baby voices, never, ever, mistake a penchant for plush with anything more sexy. Girls like soft toys. But not in that way.

You openly admit that dressing up has a sexual context for you, but, apparently, being a furry is not necessarily a sexual predilection. In fact, several of your furry brethren say that they are irritated at the increasingly widely held belief that 'fursuiting' is a sexual fetish.

Furries describe themselves as big fans of animals with human characteristics – characters who can talk, walk on two legs and use opposable thumbs – and they dress up in costume so that they can take on the physical and mental form of their chosen character. As you do. They stress that few fur suits that are sold have been adapted with sexual features. However, having had a look at www.fursuitsex.com, it's clear that one doesn't need a GCSE in domestic science to snip a handy set of holes in a Snagglepuss costume.

Under the circumstances, I think it would be naive to unload your furry little secret and expect your girlfriend to react sympathetically. Unless she is nursing a fetish of her own, the chance of her volunteering to dress up as Boo Boo and stroke your Yogi Bear is about as likely as Esperanto becoming a European tongue.

So, unless you feel that she is 'the one', you might be better off trying to find a partner who has already discovered her inner fox/bear/skunk. There is a fairly hot-looking female skunk/tiger presenting herself on You Tube. She dances provocatively by her bed, wearing a pink silk slip over her black-and-white tiger-striped body. Her skunk face has a knowing smile and her big cartoon eyes stare out at the viewer in a challenging way. She sits down on the bed, arches her back and says 'Ooooh, sexy'. In a very deep male voice.

Britain's furry community may be smaller than in the US, but there are people who share your interest. UKFur, the main website for furries in the UK, has more than 1,500 members and they arrange get-togethers in London and around the country. Apparently, the soft-toy department at Hamleys is a favourite venue.

I have long had a fetish about silky women's underwear. After 34 years of marriage and seven children, I still buy slips and stockings to wear under my normal clothes. My wife won't talk about it; I just wish she could accept my inclinations.

I bet you do, but I wouldn't hold my breath. After 34 years of marriage and seven kids, there are about two chances of your wife 'accepting' your inclinations – slim and none – and, ironically, her reticence will probably be less to do with your penchant for women's clothing and more to do with the fact that you have betrayed her by leading what she regards as a double life for more than 30 years.

Women loathe marital deception. It doesn't matter whether the guilty secret is gambling, whoring or shopping for ladies' lingerie. The furtive, sneaking, duplicitous behaviour that is required to withhold the truth from the female half of a married couple is never viewed favourably.

If you were both younger, things might be different, but at a time when your wife should be looking forward to a less stressful existence, she is struggling to keep the lid on an enormous can of worms and, inevitably, she will resent you for that.

Though she appears to be completely avoiding the subject, don't for a minute believe that she hasn't struggled to understand how, or why, the man she loves feels the need to dress in women's clothing. Cross-dressing is not a fetish that emerges fully formed at 55, so she probably feels deeply foolish that she didn't spot the signs sooner and she may also question whether she, through lack of desirability, is in some way responsible for your fetish.

To top it all, although 75 per cent of cross-dressers are actually heterosexual, men who dress as 'ladeees' are perceived as being effeminate so she probably believes that you are a homosexual, too.

You say that you wish she would talk about it, but right now, pretending it isn't happening is her only form of protection. Her denial maintains the status quo and stops the inevitable explosion of emotion that would, she anticipates, destroy the marriage and put her and the children through inconceivable public humiliation.

You can't change what you are, and it is natural for you to want your wife to understand, but you can't expect her to do so automatically. She may change in time, but right now it may be that turning a blind eye is really the best that you can expect.

Though your wife doesn't want to talk to you, she might be willing to talk to other women who have found themselves in a similar situation. The Women of the Beaumont Society is an organization that provides support and information to wives and partners of cross-dressing men. It has a website, which answers many of the most pressing questions. There is also a helpline, which provides one-to-one advice and encouragement.

My wife discovered my secret stash of bondage equipment and was devastated. How can I find the words to broach the subject and persuade her it's a good idea?

If bondage play between two consenting partners is difficult for the average person to understand, solo bondage is baffling. The idea of someone wanting to dress in rubber, don a gas mask, tie a noose around his neck and strap himself to the bedpost simply doesn't make sense. It's not just the why, it's the how. Solo bondage involves meticulous preparation and the kind of skill set that is more James Bond than Joe Bloggs. The straitjacket self-bondage rope tie definitely didn't get taught at Scouts, and although the sticky plaster, squash ball, uninflated balloons, 6 ft of pink ribbon and giant joke shop dummy sound like a *Blue Peter* script, they are not, believe me.

To the average punter, the only obvious advantage to doing this kind of thing in secret is that no one else can see how ridiculous you look. But for the solo bondage fan, the energy, the sourcing, the expense, the squirrelling away, and most of all, the clandestine and hazardous nature of the activities combine to create an incomparable adrenalin rush. There is the risk of getting caught, but there is also the risk of it all going horribly wrong. It is potentially as dangerous as physical restraint in partnered sexual bondage, with the grave exception that if things do not go according to plan, you cannot escape and there is no one to rescue you.

When the Conservative MP for Eastleigh, Stephen Milligan, was discovered dead (and naked, bar some suspenders and a pair of women's stockings) by his secretary, he had an electric cord tied around his neck, a black bin liner over his head and a piece of orange in his mouth. I suspect that his fiancée at the time was, like your wife, devastated to discover that her partner had been hiding his sexual predilections from her.

Solo bondage is a very exclusive club with a membership of one. You operate alone. You satisfy your own needs without any need to compromise, any need to accommodate anyone else. Your enthusiasm for this secret, silent and highly introspective form of stimulation probably developed years ago and I would imagine that you yourself found your interests challenging initially.

Consider then how much more complex your wife's situation is. In her eyes your involvement with bondage is a sexual commitment that does not involve her. It is a lie that you have been living under her nose and any attempt to persuade her that 'it is a good idea' is unlikely to work in your favour.

At best, your wife will view your interests as a unique kind of sexual indulgence, at worst, an enormous betrayal. In choosing to keep this part of yourself private you denied her the right to know you in full. Now that she is enlightened, she has the right to decide what she wants, in her own time and on her own terms.

9.

Oysters, aphrodisiacs & mutations in the food chain

Do some foods really act as aphrodisiacs or is that just an old wives' tale? I was planning to cook a special meal for my girlfriend and thought it would be exciting to try some foods that would get us in the mood for later, but I don't know where to start. I've heard oysters do the trick, but neither of us really likes shellfish.

Since there are few people interested in conducting clinical trials on the sexual potency of the banana, no one can say categorically that aphrodisiacs do, or don't, work.

Before the invention of the banana milkshake, the banana muffin or, my personal favourite, banoffee pie, banana consumption may well have increased libido because the fruit contains potassium and B vitamins, which are necessary for sex hormone production.

Oysters contain high quantities of zinc, which can stimulate and increase blood flow, and a scientific study unveiled at the American Chemical Society, indicated that eating oysters and other bivalves can raise the levels of sexual hormones. But how many oysters do you have to eat?

Chocolate contains phenylethylamine, an ingredient that is said to promote feelings of well-being and sexual arousal, but according to the aphrodisiac expert Amy Reiley, you'd have to eat so much chocolate to experience the effect that you would be more likely to go into a diabetic coma. Reiley, who has a degree in gastronomy and is the author of *Fork Me, Spoon Me: The Sensual Cookbook*, says that cheese contains ten times more of the same components, so you would be better off eating Stilton.

When it comes to aphrodisiacs you have to factor in a large placebo effect. If a person believes that foods have sexual properties, he or she has at least a 30 per cent chance (the placebo effect is generally about 30 per cent in clinical trials) of experiencing a boost to libido.

The beauty of aphrodisiac foods is that, while they might not do much good, they certainly won't do any harm, so it's worth giving them all a try. Oysters are obviously a good place to start. And ginger is said to stimulate the circulatory system which makes the tongue tingle, swells the lips and raises body temperature. Spicy foods, such as chillies, are thought to boost the libido by increasing your heart rate. And according to the Vegetarian Society, consumed consecutively over three days, asparagus – which contains vitamins A, C and B6, folic acid, potassium, fibre and thiamin – can have a powerful effect on libido.

If you want to create something a little special, you could try this recipe. Truffles were favoured by the Ancient Greeks who believed that their musky scent stimulated and sensitized the skin. If you can get your hands on some fresh white or black truffles, the following recipe is a simple and delicious way to start your weekend. Plan your romantic breakfast for a Saturday morning when neither you nor your partner have any commitments. On the previous Thursday, put your truffles in an airtight container with four raw eggs in their shells. By Saturday morning the truffles will have impregnated through the shells of the eggs and perfumed the egg with their aroma.

Crack the eggs into a bowl and gently whisk with a little salt and freshly ground white pepper. Then bring about 4 tablespoons of double cream to the boil in a saucepan and add a knob of butter. Add the eggs and gently stir with a wooden spoon. Meanwhile, toast some white bread. Continue to stir the eggs and remove from the heat when they are still soft and fluffy. Butter the toast and spoon on the scrambled eggs. Grate some of the truffles over the eggs and serve immediately with a glass of champagne garnished with a vanilla bean. Enjoy!

I'm 45 and want to improve my performance in bed without resorting to little blue pills. I've read about a natural supplement called yohimbine, but I'm nervous about buying anything over the internet because I wouldn't be sure what I was taking. I have also heard that watermelon has the same effect, but not on me so far. Can you separate fact from fiction?

First the boring, responsible bit. Softer erections can be caused by age, alcohol use, diabetes, kidney disease, neurological disease, lack of sleep, hormonal imbalances, stress, anxiety, guilt, depression, low self-esteem, vascular diseases such as hypertension, high cholesterol or atherosclerosis, or as a side-effect of medications.

Before experimenting with 'natural' anything, you should consult your doctor and get a clean bill of health. You should also do whatever you can to improve your circulation, including exercise and cutting out fatty foods that could be clogging your arteries, knackering your hydraulics and turning you into a tub of lard.

Though your desire to avoid chemicals is admirable, 40 per cent of prescription drugs – antibiotics, opiates, anticancer drugs, steroids, cardiac glucosides, antimalarials, statins – have natural origins, so if your doc says you are a good candidate for Viagra, weigh up the benefits before ruling it out. A natural alternative to Viagra is less likely to cause blue-tinged vision, deafness, possible infertility and, rarely, priapism – erections that won't go down – but then, a natural alternative to Viagra is less likely to work.

Although the internet is awash with recommendations for the magical sex powers of avena sativa, damiana, ginseng, ginkgo biloba, maca, muira puama and zinc, there is no credible evidence to show that any of them improve sexual function.

There is, however, evidence to support the efficacy of yohimbine. A 1996 review of 16 studies at Syracuse University, and a 1998 British analysis of seven studies, showed yohimbine to be an effective treatment for erectile dysfunction. But there is also evidence that it isn't. An analysis of 208 studies published from 1979 to 1994 led the American Urological Association to conclude that yohimbine is no better than a placebo. Side-effects include rapid heart rate, high blood pressure, insomnia, panic attacks, hallucinations, headaches, dizziness, skin flushing, seizures and renal failure. And because it can increase blood pressure to unsafe levels you can't consume it with cheese, red wine or liver.

Another supposed alternative is the amino acid L-arginine. In a study of 50 men at Tel Aviv University, 31 per cent of those with impotence found their erections had improved after six weeks of taking one gram of L-arginine three times a day. L-arginine boosts nitric oxide levels, which relaxes blood vessels and improves circulation. It was thought that these qualities might benefit patients with heart conditions; however, in 2006 a clinical trial of the supplement, headed by Dr Steven Schulman, of Johns Hopkins Medical Institutions in America, was abandoned after six cardiac patients died. No patients in the placebo group died. Other side-effects are abdominal pain, bloating, diarrhoea, gout and worsening asthma.

The good news is that Italian scientists have discovered a compound called icariin, made from *Epimedium brevicornum*, aka horny goat weed. Like sildenafil, the active ingredient in Viagra, icariin inhibits the enzyme PDE5, which increases bloodflow to the penis. Although Viagra is 80 times more effective than icariin, scientists hope that they may be able to create a more powerful synthetic molecule with no nasty side-effects. In about ten years…

Which brings us, finally, to watermelon. The pink flesh of this fruit contains compound citrulline, which converts to arginine in the body. There is no 'dosage' per se, but if you want to increase your intake try scooping out the flesh of a whole melon, chopping it into small chunks and freezing it. Then, at about 7 p.m., chuck a couple of handfuls of the frozen flesh into a blender with some fresh strawberries, a little sugar, lemon juice, a tiny splash of vodka, and half a Viagra. Delicious. And potent.

As a strict vegan is it morally acceptable for me to perform oral sex without a condom? I don't want to lose either my principles or my boyfriend.

I wasn't sure whether this was a meat or gravy issue so I called the Vegan Society for moral guidance. When I read out your question over the phone to the public relations woman, her rather flustered response was: 'Oh goodness, maybe I should get back to you on this one.' Which she did. And here, straight from the horse's mouth, if that would be appropriate, is the official party line from the Vegan Society: 'We work to promote lifestyles based on the non-consumption of animal products and don't really deal with the consumption of human animal products.' In other words, it wasn't sure either.

It did, however, recommend the lubricated Condomi condoms sold at its online shop, in slightly puzzling sizes: regular, extra large and studded. Fortunately, brushing up on veggie sex was easier elsewhere.

At *Nerve*, America's coolest, smartest, most honest sex magazine, Tana, 29, a vegan for four years, navigates herself and her principles around this thorny issue by refusing to swallow 'if the semen belongs to a guy who is not a vegan'. She has no problem with vegan semen and says that, as an aide to fellatio, a cream made from tofu is good.

At www.veganporn.com, a site that you really ought to visit, Incredible Weirdo defends a vegan's right to swallow by asking: 'How much of your own spit do you swallow everyday?' And ZoeB makes a fair point when she says that oral sex can be justified for vegans because 'animals don't consent to being eaten'.

Though you wouldn't think that taste could possibly matter to people who choose to eliminate two out of the five food groups, it does. Particularly when it comes to oral sex. Everyone at Veganporn says that vegan partners taste better (well, they would, wouldn't they?). Ryan admits that: 'I have gone down on only one vegan but I must say that her taste was far better than any carnivore. I date only vegans now.' Marie agrees: 'Honestly, my ex-boyfriend was a vegan and his semen was much sweeter than the carnivore I'm dating now. It's a completely different taste. As unbiased as I can be, just purely talking about sex the vegan boy tastes better.'

I'm not sure whether your boyfriend is vegan too but, if he is not, you might want to consider putting him on a veggie detox before you go anywhere near his penis.

The digestion of dairy products and animal flesh has deleterious effects on the taste of sperm. Mind you, so do garlic, onions, Brussels sprouts and veggie curry.

Fortunately, there are ways to sweeten bodily fluids; pineapple juice, bananas and papaya are good, as is parsley because it eliminates body odour and freshens breath, too.

Beer also sweetens the taste of semen and, fortunately, the big brands can be classified as vegan. Budweiser, Red Stripe Lager, Kirin, Cobra, Heineken Export, Hoegaarden, Rolling Rock, Beck's and Kingfisher. Though beer isn't the place you'd expect to find animal products, many are filtered with animal ingredients such as 'isinglass' (derived from fish) or 'bone char' (charcoal derived from animal bones).

The filtering process leaves only trace animal residues in the final product, but if you are experiencing a moral dilemma about whether or not to swallow your boyfriend's semen, then you sound like the kind of girl that this would matter to as well.

I am 34 and my boyfriend wants to be more experimental in bed. I quite like the idea of eating food off him, perhaps chocolate or cream. Any tips?

Vanish? Salt? Vinegar? Bleach? Practically everyone discovers an alternative use for Nutella at some stage but, sadly, the experience rarely lives up to expectations. As is always the way, the celluloid fantasy of food sex – Marlon Brando with a pound of butter in *Last Tango in Paris*, Mickey Rourke and Kim Basinger with the contents of the fridge in *9½ Weeks* – doesn't translate off screen.

In Hollywood, substances miraculously smear themselves over perfect skin in an aesthetically pleasing way and no one has to clean up afterwards. In real life you prise the crusty lid off a jar that hasn't been opened for months, dig a spoon in, plonk a dollop on to your partner's less than perfect bod and then try to coax the stiff and slightly congealed goo over his member.

This process is so unsexy that once you have squidged the spread over his bits, taking care to avoid the pubic hair, you will almost certainly have to rustle up an erection from his now flaccid penis. Then, even if you are successful in reviving his enthusiasm, by the time you are finished you are a sticky mess and the only unforgettable aspect about the experience is a nasty stain that refuses to budge from your favourite nightie.

So, if you want to experiment with food and sex my advice would be to avoid setting up something as contrived as licking chocolate off each other and concentrate on exploring the aphrodisiac effects of sensuous ingredients instead.

Though science has yet to prove or disprove the libido-enhancing properties of foods such as caviar, oysters, chocolate and champagne, does anyone really care whether it is the testosterone-boosting zinc in the shellfish, the tryptophan and phenylethylamine in the chocolate, or even just the fact that you are slightly pissed that does the trick?

The way to a man's heart is through his stomach, but if you are aiming for a target a little lower down the anatomy, you don't want to spend the night slaving over a hot stove.

Enjoying an evening of aphrodisiac delights requires a greater degree of preparation than your average evening meal. But most of it can be organized the day before and, if you keep the menu simple and make sure that you have everything you need to hand, you'll have time to style a more intimate dining environment on the day.

Forget eating at the table. Create a romantic atmosphere by setting up a picnic area on the floor, with cushions, throws and sheepskins if you have them. Surround your oasis with vanilla-scented candles and turn up the heating. You want the room to be nice and warm so that you can get undressed without getting goose pimples.

For appetizers, work with asparagus, almonds, caviar, truffles or fresh figs. Sashimi (tuna, mackerel, salmon and scallops), with pickled ginger, wasabi and warmed sake, has great taste and texture and you can't fail with the classic: buttery lobster and Laurent Perrier pink champagne (or scrimp with cava if you're on a budget).

It's messy, but feeding each other pink flesh, smearing butter over warm skin and kissing each other with a mouth full of bubbly is the most fantastically sensual experience.

For pudding, pass Green & Black's vanilla ice cream from mouth to mouth or try chocolate mousse. Way better than Nutella, I promise. Bon appetit.

My partner and I both like the idea of having sex outside or in public spaces. Have you any tips on how best to achieve this without getting into dangerous territory? We are not doing this because we want other people to see us.

There is quite a big difference between having sex outside and having sex in a public place. Both are illegal, but a couple caught copping off in the foyer of the British Library are much more likely to get cuffed than a couple who endeavour to find a more private venue. Prosecution relies on a third party onlooker getting upset and reporting you.

But if you are happened upon by an unsuspecting roof tiler or scuba diver, your efforts to avoid detection will be taken into account by the boys in blue, though you may still make the 'couple get caught with pants down' headline in your local gazette.

Now I'm not suggesting you should, but if two are planning to become one with Nature, a few practical precautions can eliminate a great deal of risk. In most places, bar the foyer of the British Library, a picnic provides a decent alibi.

Comfort is essential, so dress for the occasion.

Forget your Agent Provocateur and go commando. It saves time and makes for much easier access. Flouncy skirts and petticoats slide up easily when you are standing and create an effective tent-like disguise if sitting astride your partner.

On secluded beaches, towels can be used to provide cover, but be warned, sand down there is like having sex with a razorblade. Also, remember that responsible Nature lovers don't leave litter. The smell of used condoms covered in bodily fluids will attract animals and if eaten by cows, sheep, pigs or chickens, God knows what horrid mutation could end up in the food chain. Bring a plastic bag for your rubbish and leave no souvenirs.

Although you say you don't want other people to see you, privacy can never be guaranteed in a public place. George Orwell's *1984* is now a reality in every town and city, and digital technology means you can never assume that there will be no film in the cameras.

However, at least with CCTV footage you don't have to worry that images of you will end up online. That is not the case if you are caught in the act by a new breed of peeping Tom, who, courtesy of telephoto lenses can invade your privacy and broadcast the result to millions over the internet.

Some websites feature thousands of unsuspecting couples and individuals who have been snapped unawares in compromising positions. The majority of those people will never find out that their naked butt is being downloaded on a daily basis, but since you are entertaining the idea of sex in a public place it is worth bearing in mind that just because you can't see anyone doesn't mean that no one can see you.

Although the majority of people would be horrified to think that they were being watched or filmed secretly, a certain number of people get off on the idea.

Dogging, a particularly British form of exhibitionism registered in national consciousness recently when Stan Collymore, the former England, Liverpool and Aston Villa player, admitted a penchant for the sport. Doggers (men who use walking the dog as an excuse to hang around in car parks) look for stationary cars that have their interior lights on. This signal indicates that the couple inside are doing more than getting their seatbelts on. The doggers gather round the car and watch their performance through the increasingly steamy windows and if they get lucky there is a spot of audience participation, too.

If you fancy it, the ever helpful internet provides up-to-date nationwide listings of what goes on in specific car parks around the country. If you don't, consider the fact that having sex in the privacy of your own home means that you don't have to worry about policemen, bugs, nettles, dogs, cameras or overexcited footballers.

I was caught short while on a walk with my husband. I squatted in the bushes while he guarded me and, oddly, I found the experience very arousing. Is this normal?

Arousal is not an instinct that we can control. The urge to have sex often springs upon us when we least expect it. It can sometimes be explained by unintentional physical stimulation; for example, from the vibrations of a bus or riding a bike.

At other times it sneaks in through the back door while we are daydreaming, studying or just plain bored. It can be triggered by drugs, smells, hormones, images, music, the words of Shakespeare or the taste of salty sweat. It is an indefinable and endlessly curious state. And although squatting in the bushes wouldn't necessarily do it for everyone, the combination of sensations you describe does sound peculiarly erotic. The fear of discovery. The adrenalin rush of undressing in a public place. The complicity you felt with your husband as protector. The intimacy between you and your husband as voyeur. And the ecstasy of releasing an overloaded bladder. Frankly, that's more than just an emergency pee; that's a damned sexy experience.

So rather than worry about whether it is normal, why not see if you can use the sensations you describe to add something to your sexual repertoire. Though I wouldn't normally quote George Michael, you might consider taking a leaf out of his book, or rather his song 'Outside': 'I think I'm done with the sofa./ I think I'm done with the hall./ I think I'm done with the kitchen table, baby./ Let's go outside (let's go outside)/ in the sunshine./ I know you want to, but you can't say yeah.'

Mr Michael was famously less concerned about the legal implications of his behaviour than you might be. There are laws that protect members of the public from being unwilling witnesses to sexual behaviour. Basically, something has to constitute a 'gross act of indecency' before it merits arrest and you will be prosecuted only if you are reported by a third party. So if you and your husband find a location where you wouldn't expect to be spied on, you can probably commune with nature quite safely.

If you are scared of getting caught, a practical approach and appropriate attire can eliminate much of the risk. Discomfort is a factor that most people forget when getting it on outdoors. Put a thick blanket between you and Mother Earth to avoid scratches, stings, poking twigs, bug bites, cowpats, etc. And remember, responsible nature lovers don't leave any litter.

Some couples like to remember their outdoor exploits by visually recording them for private perusal. Others generously share their adventures with the world by posting their pictures online, such as on Voyeurweb. But a quick glimpse at this fascinating, if slightly disturbing, website reveals how dangerous it is to ever presume that you are completely alone.

10.

Talking dirty, aural sex & stuffing a sock in it

I am a woman in my early 40s and have always enjoyed sex. My new partner is great in bed but he constantly talks dirty and it turns me off. What to do?

There is a strong argument to be made for men being forced to take an exam in creative discourse before they're allowed to 'talk dirty' because most male attempts at verbal arousal leave women wanting to stuff a sock in their mouth. Maybe it is because men are not as narrative-orientated as women.

According to the National Literacy Trust, boys perform worse than girls in all literacy related tasks and tests, and most women would agree that this is a discrepancy that never really resolves itself. Although men don't appear to have much of an affinity with words, research (and, let's face it, personal experience) shows that they respond well to images.

Edward O. Laumann, in the US's biggest sex survey (*Sex, Love and Health in America*, 2000), reported that men are four times more likely to look at sexually explicit material than women and they don't like to waste time with text, preferring pictures that leave little to the imagination. Needless to say, this does nothing to improve their erotic idiom. The standard sexual script of group fantasies, or threat of intent, are usually lifted from the porn mag they've just been reading and, for women, it's as exciting as shopping with toddlers in tow.

Talking dirty works only if it is seductive, if it drags a woman into a relevant erotic script and makes her feel that she is colluding in a fantasy with a partner who has managed to decode her hidden desires. No, I've never met a man who could do that either, but for those who want to learn, it's the difference between: 'I'm taking off your stockings because I realize I've been much too lenient with you, my little vixen'; and 'I'm going to strip you naked and f*** you'. Both statements essentially say the same thing but one entices while the other offends (that's the second one, guys). Unfortunately, few men seem able to intuit this subtle distinction. Although lots of women hate it when their man breaks out in X-rated vocabulary, they can't bring themselves to say anything to him at the time. Instead of whispering 'Shhh' or sticking their tongue in his mouth, they let their poor unsuspecting partner hang himself, oblivious that every word he utters tightens the noose.

Ironically, this is just old-fashioned female insecurity. Women worry that if they express their distaste they'll come across as uptight or prudish, so they bite their lips. Which is absurd, really, because men are not as judgmental as women and most guys would be grateful to be told that the script they have been delivering for years has been going down like a lead balloon.

The other aspect that women find frightening is the thought of having the tables turned on them. If they criticize their partners' verbal talents they risk being asked to put their money where their mouth is, and they fear that they wouldn't be any better. It creates a classic sexual impasse: he doesn't know what she wants so he presses on and hopes for the best; she doesn't know how to express what it is that she wants so she says nothing and lies back thinking of England.

Fortunately, it is a quandary that can be rectified by anyone with a good grasp of the two big C words: communication and co-operation. If you want the French singer Serge Gainsbourg tickling your fancy not the porn movie star Ron Jeremy taking you prisoner, it's up to you to say so. Or, stuff a sock in your own mouth. He'll get the message, eventually.

My husband wants to spice up our love life. He has suggested that we talk dirty, but I can think of nothing more embarrassing. I was quite happy with our sex life but now I feel as though he is bored and that perhaps I am not the person he should be with. Should I go along with it or say that it's just not me?

Unfortunately, even in the most secure sexual relationship, a request by one partner to 'spice things up' has a 50-50 chance of being interpreted as a criticism. Make those odds 90-10 if anyone is foolish enough to mention the word boring, in any context whatsoever.

It is natural that you should feel sensitive, defensive even, but don't reject your husband for attempting to keep the sexual spark alight. All long-term relationships require reinvention and rejuvenation, and if suggestions for change are automatically dismissed, then stagnation is inevitable. And remember, if your husband felt that he was with the wrong person he wouldn't bother trying to invest in your sexual relationship. Even though you are not enthusiastic about his proposal, try to accept that he means well.

Having said that, I couldn't agree with you more. I've always felt that women who can multi-task writhing with breathy utterings of 'Oooh, you're so big and hard' in bed, deserve an Oscar.

And when men attempt to talk dirty, their efforts reveal either a startling lack of imagination or a sexuality that is informed by porny websites. I suspect that the main reason most women don't engage with sex talk is because we have, in our time, delivered enough lies from compromised positions to know that the reward is generally the sound of snoring.

And that's not much of a motivation, to be honest.

Most women who feel uncomfortable about talking dirty agree that existing interpretations of that particular skill are so soiled by 'the language of porn' that 'the language of sex' seems to have been forgotten. And there really is a world of difference between the two.

It's not just about vocabulary – although avoiding terminology that demeans or depersonalizes is a good start – it's about relevance. The popular model of sex, seen in adverts and on television, is so far-removed from what goes on in the average domestic bedroom that imposing X-rated dialogue on what is essentially sex under a John Lewis duvet feels, understandably and undeniably, wrong.

So, instead of adopting the humiliating prose of porn, what you and your husband need to do is to write your own sexual script. The easiest way to do this is to take your cues from what you like doing with each other, and then feed the information back to each other.

However, if you are genuinely shy you may want to try the following exercise. Get naked with your husband, switch off the lights and lie down side by side. You can't touch each other. Now, quietly discuss the kind of sex you like to have with each other; what you like him to do to you; what he likes you to do to him.

Keep the conversation grounded in reality. No fiction. No theatricals. You are not talking dirty, you are just talking, but you'll find, within about five minutes, that in the same way that making a statement such as 'I really need a coffee' makes you really, really want a coffee, the simple combination of honest erotic description and heightened sexual anticipation creates a powerful sexual charge. And then, when you can't bear it any longer, you can make it all happen for real. Fun, isn't it?

My boyfriend makes whimpering noises when we have sex. I find it a real turn-off but I don't know how to tell him without hurting his feelings or ruining the moment completely. I really like him and don't want this issue to ruin our relationship.

Because 'copulatory vocalization' – that's the scientific term for the noises people make during sex – is presumed to be involuntary, it is excused as something that 'he can't help', but it isn't involuntary and he can help it.

Though Hollywood begs us to believe otherwise, men and women do not need to grunt like Neanderthals when they are in the throes of passion.

Studies into copulatory vocalization may not seem like the best use of the limited scientific research budget but, fortunately for you, Dr Gayle Brewer, of the University of Central Lancashire, and the psychologist Colin Hendrie, of the University of Leeds, managed to complete a paper entitled 'Evidence to Suggest that Copulatory Vocalizations in Women are Not a Reflexive Consequence of Orgasm', before anyone noticed how insane the topic was.

The study documents the responses of 71 women between 18 and 48 who were asked everything everyone never needed to know about the noises that people make during sex. The results of the study established that 66 per cent of the women used copulatory vocalization as a way of manipulating the speed of their partner's ejaculation. While female orgasms were most commonly experienced during foreplay, copulatory vocalizations were made most often 'before and simultaneously with male ejaculation.'

Brewer and Hendrie's data was found to be remarkably

consistent with findings reported in non-human primates such as Barbary macaque monkeys, which found that the likelihood of male ejaculation is directly related to the intensity and speed of female vocalizations during copulation.

I suspect that if female macaque monkeys could talk, their explanations for this behaviour would differ little from those offered by their human counterparts. The women in the Brewer and Hendrie study cited discomfort, boredom, fatigue and 'time limitations' as their reasons for using noise to hasten sexual climax. Yet, despite the apparent negative connotations of these rationalizations, 92 per cent of the women questioned felt very strongly that their vocalizations boosted their partner's self-esteem and 87 per cent reported using them for this purpose.

While there is no parallel male study, it is obviously not inconceivable that a man might also make noises during sex if he believes that it will heighten arousal. For example, if a former girlfriend told your boyfriend that she thought that the noises he made during sex were cute, and you have never said anything to the contrary, then why would he not carry on with the behaviour?

You should have been straight with him from the start because issues such as this are best tackled as soon as they are encountered. However, there are ways of communicating your dissatisfaction without hurting his feelings. Have you tried whimpering back? It just might work. Or you could try the psychological strategy known as 'operant conditioning' – teaching human beings, and other animals, to make an association between a behaviour and a consequence. In other words, a person can learn to voluntarily perform in a certain way in order to earn a reward. For example, a child can be motivated to do well in school if good reports garner praise, and a dog can be persuaded to stay and sit if he receives a chocolate drop. Similarly, a boyfriend can be taught to associate whimpering with sexual interruption. Every time he starts whimpering, you stop stimulating him; and when he stops making annoying noises, you carry on. If he starts squeaking again, you stop. He'll work it out eventually.

My girlfriend screams when we make love and my neighbours can hear us. This has a detrimental effect on my erection. How can I shut her up?

Have you tried asking her? I know it is hard to believe, but sometimes good old-fashioned face-to-face verbal communication is more effective than a letter to *The Times*. Even if your girlfriend is oblivious to the fact that she makes a lot of noise during sex, as her partner you are entitled to raise this subject.

Explain to her how it makes you feel and ask her – in as nice a way as possible – to turn down the volume. You have a right to tell her that although your ego greatly enjoys the sound of her screaming, the 'people pleaser' inside you is paranoid about disturbing your elderly neighbours, or even giving them a bad impression about the kind of things you get up to in private.

It does seem strange that two people can feel completely relaxed about getting naked, having sex and even sharing a post-coital fag and yet not feel secure enough to be able to communicate something as simple as the word 'Shh' to the person in bed beside them. In a world where the subject of sex is omnipresent; where people of all ages are equipped with sophisticated sexual vocabularies; where manuals and movies and magazines tell people what to do, and how to do it better; where there is an enormous, burgeoning wealth of information and advice on the subject of sex available, it seems contradictory that people are in relationships where they don't feel comfortable to negotiate the simple stuff such as wanting him to use a condom or her to stop screaming or even whether it is OK to fart in bed?

I hold out a faint hope that your letter is an attempt to find the right words to tell your girlfriend how you feel without hurting her. The sentence 'How can I shut her up?' does not fill me with confidence. Sensitivity might not be your strong point, but if you are to get your message across without damaging your relationship, you will need to speak to your girlfriend in a language that she understands.

Men and women communicate in different ways. Studies indicate that when men speak they tend to give information or to report. They talk about things rather than people. They convey facts, not details. They are goal-oriented. They focus on solving problems and are less likely to ask for help or directions. Men compete.

Women, on the other hand, talk to get information and to connect or to gain rapport. They talk about people rather than things. They convey feelings. They are relationship-oriented. They are quicker to ask for, and to accept, help or directions. Women co-operate.

These differences can create conflict, particularly when couples are trying to discuss sensitive issues. If your girlfriend is told that her screaming is wrong, or inappropriate, or embarrassing; if you report your dissatisfaction in a factual and logical fashion; if you make the problem solely hers, then you will almost certainly leave her feeling humiliated and hurt, and her instinct will be to withdraw from you.

Instead present the issue in a more emotional way, choose an appropriate moment and reassure her that you love her and the sex you have together. Explain that the anxiety you feel is making you feel less confident about your performance. If you can own the problem with her, then you can sort it out together, and your relationship will be all the stronger for it.

My boyfriend travels a lot and wants to have telephone sex. We tried once, but I just felt stupid. How can I keep my dignity and keep him happy?

With difficulty. Unless you are a poet, words spoken into a lump of plastic are a clumsy replacement for the subtleties of sex. Minus eye-contact, graphic descriptions of body parts and what one might do with them become an uncomfortable union of GCSE biology and bad porn, so it's not surprising that you felt stupid. Few people are equipped with the kind of vocabulary required for convincing phone sex. In fact, as late-night TV adverts for phone sex lines prove, sex chat is a skill that eludes even those that get paid to provide it.

Unfortunately for you, even if you could learn to imitate the breathy tones of a 'hot 'n' horny busty blonde', you would still have to deal with the fact that you actually have a relationship with your boyfriend.

Professional phone sex works only because the client and the operator don't know each other. The connection is purely a business contract and it is all on the client's terms. He calls when he feels like it. She says what he wants to hear. He masturbates to orgasm and pays the phone bill. A proper couple can't emulate that 'unrelationship' unless they disconnect from each other, which shoots intimacy in the foot and, in your case, defeats the purpose of engaging in phone sex in the first place. You are trying to sustain your relationship and, unlike the hot 'n' horny busty blonde, you will sign off your phone call by telling him that you love him and passing on a message from his mum.

Paid-for phone sex ends when you hang up. Phone sex with the one you love has the potential to linger like a bad smell. Because the 'only limit is your imagination', too often participants make the mistake of coming over all creative.

At best this means not letting reality get in the way of a good story; for example, disregarding the fact that it is impossible to suck someone's toes while taking them from behind. At worst, it opens a can of worms. Introduce whips and chains to a partner who, unbeknownst to you, has ideological issues with the concept of domination, and you can expect the other end of the line to go silent for all the wrong reasons. Suggest three-way fantasy sex with your favourite celebrity when your other half is paranoid about infidelity and you ensure at least three frosty interrogations about whether you really would join the mile-high club with George Clooney if you were fortuitously seated next to him after an unexpected upgrade.

Knowing and then respecting each other's sexual boundaries is important if you are going to try phone sex again and if you can establish a level of explicitness that you both feel comfortable with, then you won't say anything that will cause offence. If you still feel that you can't find the words to conjure up a convincing erotic fantasy, then perhaps you should consider using someone elses.

Next time your boyfriend travels, tuck a copy of *Bedtime Stories for Women*, by Nancy Madore, into his suitcase and have him read you an erotic fairytale every night. Return the favour by reading to him from *Five-Minute Erotica*, by Carol Queen. Another collection worth looking at is *Best of Best Women's Erotica*, edited by Marcy Sheiner.

Reading from a text means that neither of you has to take responsibility for the sexual scenarios being presented, which may alleviate some of the embarrassment for you. Or not. There is only one way to find out …

11.

Birth, bonding & the last nail in the sexual coffin

My girlfriend of five years and I are trying to have a baby, but it has been ten months of trying and that is taking its toll on our relationship. I feel like a turkey-baster on legs, having to 'produce' on demand. Sex has become a chore rather than a pleasure and I don't know how much longer I can do it for. Any suggestions?

In *Breathe: A Guy's Guide to Pregnancy*, by Mason Brown, there is an amusingly twisted little graph that illustrates how the odds of conception are inversely proportional to its desirability. At the peak of the chart are unwed teenage boys who get girls pregnant if they look twice at them. At the base are financially secure married men hoping for children who are doomed to spend their weekends in fertility clinics masturbating into cups.

When you cast your mind back over a sexual history dominated by condom use and finger-crossing, the indignity of 'producing on demand' is doubly infuriating. All those university pregnancy scares were wasted angst and now, when you want her to pee two blue lines it refuses to happen. Though it's a secret best confined to the eight remaining people in Britain who qualify for a mortgage, it is quite difficult to get pregnant. For every 100 couples having sex two to three times a week, about 30 will conceive within one month, 60 will be pregnant within six months and 85 will have conceived within a year.

When a couple first make the decision to try for a baby there is huge expectation, but by the time that foreplay involves ovulation kits, calendars, secretions and temperature charts, men begin to feel that they are being used. Inevitably this has a deleterious effect on a couple's sex life. The combined frustrations of paranoia and passion-killing persistence are enough to dampen the enthusiasm of any potential parent, but, if it is any consolation, you and your girlfriend are not at the point where you should be concerned about infertility.

If your girlfriend was on the Pill before you started trying, rule out the first three months because her ovulation would have been all over the place. And if you have been using an ovulation kit and waiting until she has ovulated, you need to pull your timing back by a day or two because sperm can live for several days inside the body. Having sex before ovulation occurs gives the little fellows time to travel up the Fallopian tubes and lie in wait for the egg.

You also need to have sex every other day because storing up sperm for longer than three days is detrimental to its quality. You should be doing everything you can to maximize your chances of conceiving naturally because assisted fertility is a nightmare. If you and your girlfriend went to a doctor tomorrow you would probably be advised to start having tests and, regardless of the results, you would start to believe that there was something wrong. That anxiety would further scupper your chances and you would, as Mason Brown points out, soon find yourself masturbating into a sterile jar in a hospital cubicle.

Infertility is big business in Britain, but Zita West, one of Britain's best-known fertility experts, admits that 50 per cent of the couples she sees in her practice have nothing wrong with them apart from that they don't understand ovulation and they don't have enough sex.

Stop worrying, take a month off work, go on an amazing holiday with your girlfriend, and forget about the whole thing. Though I have absolutely no scientific evidence to support this advice, three couples who were friends of mine did just that and it certainly put the spark back into their relationships. One couple who had given up on IVF and were resigned to being childless went scuba diving. Another couple spent the money they had put aside for just-in-case IVF on a Caribbean holiday. And a third friend who had not used contraception since she got married, travelled to New Zealand with her husband. All three couples came back with an extra passenger on board.

My wife had a baby three months ago and she still won't have sex with me. I'm trying to be patient, but I'm getting desperate. Could something be wrong?

Of course there is something wrong. Three months ago, your wife pushed a baby the size of a watermelon out of her tiny vagina and for nine months before that her body was pumped chock full of killer hormones designed to attack counterproductive parenting characteristics, such as the desire to diet, exercise, get wildly drunk or have rampant sex.

Pregnancy is Nature's way of annihilating the female ego to ensure that a woman is fully primed for her role as a 24-hour milk slave to a baby that plans to dine at all hours for the first six months of its life. Over a period of 40 weeks, pregnancy breaks down even the most resistant woman and after the birth the torture of no sleep further obliterates any sense of perspective. Self-esteem becomes babycentric. A single smile makes up for the fact that a woman's once pert breasts have become pendulous milk jugs. And because baby wants to be held all the time, and leakages and spit-ups make getting dressed pointless, even the most immaculately groomed woman finds herself spending whole days plodding around in her nightie or watching daytime telly with her boobs hanging out to aerate her chapped nipples.

Exhausted, the woman who once fought furiously to stay a size ten fuels herself on chocolate biscuits and takeaways, and turns a blind eye to the baby weight that stubbornly refuses to shift. So tired. And so beyond caring.

Motherhood is meant to 'come naturally' to women. And it does. But that doesn't mean that it is easy. No matter how well prepared a woman feels, how many books she read and antenatal classes she attended, becoming a mother for the first time is like being run over by an emotional steamroller. Once the baby is born everything goes on hold until the snapper is robust enough to make it through the night. A new mother is constantly alert, and wiped out. Every ounce of energy and emotion is targeted towards her baby. She cares so much about her newborn that she will sacrifice anything for the welfare of the tiny defenceless scrap, even her relationship with her husband. As you can testify.

Your wife has been hypnotized by 8 lb of Babygro with a button nose and you feel, understandably, shafted. It's not fair. And you do have conjugal rights, but you can't reason with biology. No matter how desperate you feel, until she cuts the umbilical cord she will continue to feel about as sexual as a bowl of cold porridge. The process of withdrawal usually begins with weaning, but depending on the woman, that can take anything from six months to 60 years. In the meantime, the only way to muscle in and stop the cosy twosome alienating you from your own home is to actively involve yourself in the affair. Not only is this the fastest and most effective way to get back into your wife's field of vision, it is a surprisingly seductive and rewarding experience in itself.

Men who engage with their children while they are babies bond more strongly with them, but unfortunately, although new mothers like to broadcast how tiring everything is, they are often remarkably reluctant to share the responsibility with anyone else. If your wife resists your efforts to get involved, persist, because it will be the Athena-poster vision of your manly torso cradling your baby's soft skin that makes her rediscover her sexual feelings for you. Well, that and the fact that she is already planning a little brother or sister...

After giving birth to three children my vagina has lost its muscle tone. My partner finds it difficult to reach orgasm inside me and I feel that I should do something about it before our sex life deteriorates any further.

If my own experience is anything to go by, pregnancy involves a constant stream of badgering about Dr Arnold Kegel and his pelvic-floor exercises (the rhythmic clenching and unclenching of the pubococcygeal, PC, muscles). I recall bright-eyed and bushy-tailed midwives encouraging me to 'do them while I was waiting for the bus', and junior doctors who looked too young to have ventured beyond tonsil-hockey earnestly stressing the importance of staying 'honeymoon fresh'. And the only time I ever saw a gynaecologist, I was warned that in nine months' time I would push out both my baby and my sex life if I didn't 'Kegel' 50 times a day.

It was great advice and I've no doubt that the exercises work but, well, we're not very good at preventive measures are we? I mean, if we were, the birth rate would go right down, wouldn't it? And none of us would ever need to go on a diet, or pay a parking fine, or take a hangover cure.

Despite being fully informed as to what is good or right, we still tend to do what we want. And a pregnant woman with two screaming toddlers doesn't generally 'want' to stand at a bus stop trying to squeeze a lemon with her genitals. Besides which, by the time she feels her pelvic muscles giving up the ghost she has vowed never to have sex again anyway. Sick and tired of being preached to by medics, midwives and mothers-in-law, she gives Dr Kegel the intellectual finger and eats another cream bun.

It is only when her brain cells have resumed normal function and her shell-shocked body has had a full night's sleep that her dormant libido begins to yawn and stretch and flex its wasted muscle.

At that point Dr Kegel laughs in his grave and says 'I told you so', while she scribbles a message to 'PC' on a Post-it Note and sticks it on the fridge beside the diet plan and the penalty notice for the unpaid parking fines.

Fortunately, it is never too late to start and one month of clench and release 50 times a day should make a real difference. You should get your husband to do them, too, because as men age their testosterone level shrivels and so does everything else.

If you don't feel any improvement, you might want to invest in a pelvic toner. It looks like a cross between a vibrator and a set of curling tongs and the idea is that you slather it with lubricant, insert it and squeeze your PC muscles to bring the two sides together.

Alternatively, you could try Betty Dodson's Barbell. Dodson is a renowned sexologist and her stainless steel barbell is apparently 'sturdy enough to become a family heirloom that can be passed down from grandmother to granddaughter'. The mind boggles. The barbell is 15 cm (6 in) long, natch, weighs nearly 0.45 kg (1 lb) and is inserted into the vagina so that you can bench-press your PC muscles around it.

If home helps don't work, you should talk to your GP. He or she may suggest options such as 'neuromuscular electrical stimulation' (probe, electric current, vagina, muscle contraction, etc) or 'magnetic field treatment' (chair, magnets, vagina, your guess is as good as mine). As a last resort, you could always buy yourself a 'designer vagina'. It's an expensive and painful option that is likely to put you off sex for years. Which makes it a bit like childbirth really.

12.

Aesthetics, insecurities & sex with the lights out

My girlfriend has several stray hairs on her nipples which I find off-putting. Do you think I should risk saying something about it?

Several? The dictionary definition of that word is 'more than two, but fewer than many'. Which, I guess, means about five, tops ten, so we are not talking beard here. You've probably got as many or more hairs on your own nips, but somehow, on a woman, body hair seems different. Why is that? How come a handful of hairs means that your girlfriend's breasts don't conform to your notion of loveliness?

In case you don't realize it, the shaved, waxed, lasered ideal that you see on page 3 or in *Playboy* is an artifice. Real women have body hair. Tons of it. On their arms. On their legs. Under their arms. Under their pants. Even on their nipples. But men rarely get to see it.

Remember the media uproar that followed the flash of Julia Roberts's hairy armpits at the premiere of *Notting Hill*? That response is a perfect if rather disturbing illustration of quite how ingrained the relationship between hairlessness and feminity has become in our society. It began in the 1920s when the Wilkinson Sword Company doubled its razor sales with an advertising campaign claiming that female underarm hair was unfeminine and unhygienic.

If that argument had been valid it would have applied equally to both genders. Historically, men have not responded to sales tactics that prey on insecurity and vanity. Women, on the other hand, have a bankable track record when it comes to supporting industries with a vested interest in keeping them dissatisfied with themselves.

Though questions are often asked, if seldom answered, as to why women are willing to spend so much money on body-altering behaviours such as dieting and cosmetic surgery, hair removal is so common that no one ever bothers to question it.

Body hair may be a natural indicator of physical maturity, but 92 per cent of women feel obliged to get rid of it. In an Australian study that examined the motivation for hair removal, the two most highly rated reasons given by a group of secondary school girls were 'body hair is ugly' and 'men prefer women without body hair'.

Your negative reaction suggests that they are right. And that's wrong, isn't it? It's wrong that 92 per cent of women feel that they have to alter their body because their partner doesn't like the way it looks. And it is wrong that this belief has created a hair-removal market worth £280 million a year in the UK.

In this context, can you see that the handful of hairs on your girlfriend's nipples represent a statement of intent. She knows that they are there, but chooses not to get rid of them. In so doing, she is one of a minuscule 8 per cent of women ballsy enough not to conform and brave enough to believe that a woman should not be judged by her decision to leave her body the way God intended it to be.

As for whether you should say anything to her? It's entirely up to you, but if you do, I suspect that it will be you and not her nipple hair that gets the chop.

My girlfriend has the most beautiful FF breasts. She knows I adore them but she is fed up with other men staring. I tell her she should be flattered but she is now seriously considering a breast reduction operation. She says her breasts restrict her and weigh her down, but the operation sounds brutal. I love her the way she is and I am worried that I won't feel the same about her afterwards. How can I persuade her to change her mind?

She's talking about a smaller bra, not a frontal lobotomy. If going down a couple of cup sizes could negatively affect the way you feel about your girlfriend, date a porn mag. Though it is difficult for those who don't possess them to understand, 'weapons of mass seduction' are a mixed blessing. Other men staring at your girlfriend may be an ego trip for you, but have you any idea how intrusive it is to have 50 per cent of the population feel they have a right to pass remarks on your body as you walk down the street? Even Barbara Windsor says that, as a teenager, she hated walking past building sites and having 'Oi, when did you last see your feet?' yelled at her.

Yet to many women the attention forced on big-breasted women seems desirable. In one year, 8,449 women in the UK paid thousands each to have their breasts enlarged, but another 3,522 women paid roughly the same to have theirs reduced. People always want what they can't have, but while breast enlargement is largely about vanity and insecurity, reduction is usually about improving quality of life. A DD reduction to a C cup will remove about 0.5 kg (1 lb) of tissue from each breast. An FF reduction to a C cup removes almost 2 kg (4 lb). If you want to know what it feels like to carry that kind of weight around, get a couple of kilo bags of rice, stick them in one of your girlfriend's bras and wear it around the house for a day. See how they get in the way? Feel how the bra strap cuts into your shoulders? Now walk down the street and notice how everyone stares at your chest. I rest your girlfriend's case.

Rajiv Grover, a consultant plastic surgeon and secretary of the British Association of Aesthetic Plastic Surgeons, says that your girlfriend's reduction 'might be considered on medical grounds if she has symptoms related to the weight of her breasts'. This means she could potentially get the surgery free on the NHS. He advises her to 'have a full consultation so she understands the outcome, the risks and the recovery time' and adds that 'cosmetic surgery is a life-changing decision and should not be taken lightly'.

Breast reduction is, as you say, a brutal operation. The surgery takes up to four hours and means repositioning the nipples and areolas. Although surgeons try to keep them attached to their blood vessels and nerves, sometimes they have to be removed completely, which can result in a loss of sensation. In rare cases the nipple dies and has to be rebuilt from grafted skin. The operation leaves anchor-shaped scars under each breast and can prevent a woman from breastfeeding in the future.

Since she hasn't yet had children, your girlfriend should try dieting and regular upper body workouts before she investigates surgery. And you? You should quit thinking about yourself. Your girlfriend needs to know that you love her for who she is, not the size of her chest. If that distinction was more evident, she might feel more confident about her beautiful breasts.

I've recently separated from my husband after 13 years of marriage, and have started seeing a 27-year-old I met at the gym (I'm 38). He's a lovely bloke, neither of us are looking for anything serious, but we recently had sex for the first time, and he was shocked by what he considered as my lack

of grooming, compared to women of his own age that he's dated. I do look after myself (hence the gym) and I don't think that a permanent San Tropez tan and a Brazilian wax should be deal-breakers in a relationship. Or am I just hopelessly outdated?

Things have rather changed in the genital grooming department, I'm afraid, and some people feel that we have porn to thank for all of it. Sheila Jeffreys, the author of *Beauty and Misogyny: Harmful Cultural Practices in the West*, puts it bluntly when she says 'the main reason women wax their genitals appears to be the desire to please the kind of partners who find the look of pornography and prostitution sexually exciting'.

And an article entitled 'What Your Bikini Waxer Really Thinks', published in Australian *Cosmopolitan*, provides us with some insight into the male perspective. It quotes a 28-year-old accountant called Rodney, who describes the Brazilian wax as 'just the right balance of slutty and sexy, bad girl and sweet. That she would go through the pain and lavish so much attention on herself down there is so cool – and the fact that it is partly on my behalf is very exciting.'

Even Rodney is a bit outdated now, though.When he was a teenager the web was in its infancy, but by the time your boyfriend hit puberty his entire generation were using free online porn as their primary source of sex education, and, as we all know, porn stars don't have any hair down there.

It wasn't always that way. During the 1970s everyone, even your porn star, was hairy, but by the 1980s the natural look of *The Joy of Sex* was over. Porn went hardcore and hairlessness became a requirement for its stars.

Nearly 30 years later, the indirect result of close-up porn is a proliferation of waxing salons on every high street. Grooming down there is now considered to be normal, on a par with manicures, blow-drying and eyebrow waxing.

Indeed, any woman who dares to be less rigid in her styling, as you have found, risks being labeled as bucolic, unsanitary or possibly French, in which case it is usually excused – although on an episode of *The Graham Norton Show*, Gordon Ramsay revealed that this was the very reason why a former girlfriend had put him off Frenchwomen for good.

There is something hugely irritating about being forced to conform to an aesthetic ideal instigated and perpetuated by the porn industry, but, like keeping one's armpits and legs smooth, it is now expected. If your boyfriend has been conditioned to expect a tidy Brazilian, he may genuinely find anything else very off-putting.

Though the feminist ethos of your 'take me as I am' argument is perfectly valid, your boyfriend's reaction is instinctive – and in the face of something that is honestly perceived as a turn-off by one partner, rational arguments simply do not work. The good news is that, as 'issues' go, this is a pretty small one and, hey, if the relationship doesn't work out you can return to your old ways.

The bad news is that shaving sensitive areas is problematic – you are likely to leave a lot of razor bumps and create ingrown hairs. The most popular solution, waxing, is a uniquely painful experience. Imagine burning-hot, extra-strength Sellotape being ripped from delicate skin… and now treble the pain. Sadly, high-tech alternatives are not pain-free either. According to the New York Laser Clinic, laser hair-removal doesn't hurt 'that much' and feels more like being 'pinched'. You'll need up to six sessions, and the success rate is determined by the level of contrast between the colour of your hair and the colour of your skin.

Fortunately, the craze for Brazilians is abating. The hot new haircut is the Sicilian. It is like a Brazilian, but you are left with a neat little Sicily-shaped triangle, which at least means that you still look like a woman.

My boyfriend likes to have sex doggy-style in front of the mirror. Both the position and the mirror make me very uncomfortable – should I tell him?

If it is any consolation, you are not the only woman who allows vanity to limit her sexual repertoire. Once, while I was crawling around trying to pick random bits of Lego out of the shagpile carpet, I found myself kneeling over a shatterproof mirror, which I bought for my twins when they were babies. Lordy, what a shocker. Gravity had pulled all the skin on my face away from my bone structure but my eyes remained recessed in my skull like little piggy jewels.

As I watched the flesh that was once my face flap around like some hideous NASA experiment, I vowed never to go on top in bed unless my husband was wearing a blindfold. Another girl I know installed one of those wall-to-wall mirrored wardrobes in her bedroom and, as a result, became acutely self-conscious about the way she looked when having sex. She now confines herself to the missionary position because it inverts her stomach and makes her look about 5 kg (10 lb) lighter. You might want to suggest this as an alternative because it also makes you look prettier.

Where gravity drags a woman down when she is on top, it gives her a beauty boost when she is lying back and thinking of pentapeptides.

Doggy in front of the mirror is probably the ultimate challenge to any woman's self-esteem. Most women are too self-conscious about their bodies to enjoy the sight of their partner thrusting into their XL rear end while their spare tyre and nipples graze the duvet.

We wish it weren't so, but the majority of women feel so insecure about their bodies that it interferes with their ability to enjoy sex. A *Grazia* magazine survey established that 98 per cent of British women hate their bodies and that the average woman worries about her body once every 15 minutes. Indeed, a recent survey of 3,500 women by the bathroom company Shuc, revealed that a third of women think they are too fat to appear naked in front of their partners.

A few years ago the magazine *Psychology Today* carried out a survey on body image and of the 3,452 women who responded, 15 per cent said they would sacrifice more than five years of their lives to be the weight they want; 24 per cent said that they would give up more than three years. Which is 100 per cent crazy, right? If men don't notice that you have had your hair done or are wearing a nice new dress, why would they notice that your spare tyre wobbles when you go on top. The male brain tends to perform tasks predominantly with the left side, the logical/rational side of the brain. Women, on the other hand, use both sides of their brains which means that they can transfer data between the right and left hemispheres faster than men.

In sexual terms it means that an aroused man thinks of sex alone, while his multi-tasking partner over-analyses their relationship, has a crisis of confidence about her body, orchestrates intimacy to limit the number of positions that will make her look like a wobbling tub of lard, has an orgasm and then reminds herself to get the Lego out of the shagpile carpet.

My wife's put on a lot of weight in the past ten years. It is affecting our love life as I no longer find her attractive. How can I tell her?

You can't. The words 'you' and 'fat' should never be used in the same sentence when addressing any woman with whom you intend to have an ongoing relationship.

Stating the indisputably obvious might make you feel

better, but take it from me, your wife already knows she is fat, and she hates herself for it. Every morning when she wakes up she feels the rolls of fat around her midriff and berates herself. As she showers and washes between the folds of her flesh she loathes herself a little more. As she brushes her teeth, she spits toothpaste at the jowly bloater that stares back at her from the mirror and then she dresses in one of two outfits, both black, that she thinks make her look fractionally thinner before heading to the kitchen to begin her miserable daily battle with fat, carbohydrates and calories.

If it makes her so unhappy, why doesn't she do something about it, you ask? It's a fair point. Going on a diet and taking some exercise should be a no-brainer for all fatties, but unfortunately, the connection between intellectual masochism and physical motivation is not straightforward. Your wife may hate the size of her ass, but that won't necessarily be enough to get her off it. It is partly to do with unrealistic goals. Instead of accepting that it took her ten years to put the weight on and it might take her five to get it off, she loses heart after five weeks on a diet and winds up back where she started, except that this time she feels like a failure, too. The fact that you don't feel attracted to her has probably not gone unnoticed, but it may be something of a relief to her.

Overweight people rarely feel comfortable about physical intimacy. When Martin Binks, a clinical psychologist and director of behavioural science at Duke University, North Carolina, studied 1,210 overweight people, he found that four out of every ten reported physical problems with sex. Both men and women suffered from lack of sexual desire and enjoyment along with hampered performance.

And many reported avoiding sex entirely.

So what can you do to help? Emma Hetherington, the head of programme development at WeightWatchers, says: 'Don't dwell on your own feelings; give her some practical support instead.' You may also need to accept a modicum of responsibility. If she's cooking steak and chips for you every night, chances are she's eating steak and chips, so if she is going to diet successfully, you will need to make changes, too. The same goes for exercise. If you want her to stick with an exercise regimen, making dinner or volunteering to put the kids to bed will make it easier for her to find the time to get to the gym. Better still, go with her. A study of more than 31,000 men carried out by the Harvard School of Public Health found that men who were physically active had a 30 per cent lower risk of erectile dysfunction than men who did little or no physical activity. And a study by the University of British Columbia found that 20 minutes of exercise improved sexual response in the female participants, compared with no exercise at all.

Once your wife gets started she will find that success is self-propelling. And the good news for you is that the Duke study indicates that weight loss of as little as 10 per cent boosts confidence and improves sex.

After a lot of wine, I slept with a very nice but ugly man. The sex was surprisingly good but I don't fancy him. How can I make myself find him sexy?

Well, a couple of bottles of chardonnay would do the trick but you'd be staring at the same problem in the morning. With a hangover. You'd be faced with the harsh realities of broken capillaries, enlarged pores, pale rolls of flesh and rank breath, and when you were finished looking in the mirror you'd still have to deal with the ugly guy. Cold turkey.

Though beauty is in the eye of the beholder and looks shouldn't count, we all know that's rubbish. Looks count so much that society actively discriminates against people who don't conform to certain aesthetic standards and because the media manipulates the beauty gauge so that it automatically excludes 90 per cent of the population, the men and women who struggle with issues such as obesity, baldness, acne or disability are at an immediate disadvantage.

From childhood onwards, the beautiful get a better deal. Doors open for them. A study by economists at the National Bureau of Economic Research in Massachusetts shows that good-looking people earn close to 6 per cent more than average-looking individuals. Although good looks don't ensure success, they lubricate the mechanism by which it's achieved.

Because we are all self-conscious and want the person we have a relationship with to reflect well on us, when it comes to dating we have a tendency to judge the content by the package. It's a shallow and short-sighted approach to choosing a partner because beauty fades but personality and character remain.

Since you obviously have a good sexual connection with this nice man, and you like him as a person, accept that 'not fancying him' is to do with aesthetic prejudice and concern about what other people would think of you, then work out what is, or at least should be, more important to you. His nice or his ugly?

Since 90 per cent of pretty boys wouldn't score 'very nice and good in bed', I think you should give this guy another chance. Arrange to meet him again. Sober. Ignore the Hawaiian shirt and tweed jacket combo (sorting out a man's wardrobe is easy) and try not to put a bag over his head if you bump into a friend.

If you can get over your own issues with him and relax and engage with him you will probably find that, unlike the Jude Laws you've dated, Danny DeVito is a really good listener/ makes you laugh/has an enormous capacity for empathy and best of all, thinks that you are brilliant.

Enjoying his company doesn't mean you have to rush into dating him but you may find yourself looking forward to his calls or e-mails. Eventually you'll introduce him to your friends and although they'll think he's no oil painting at first, when they get to know him and realize how damn nice he is, some of them might find him attractive. The realization that other women can see beyond his appearance will help you to understand that though looks count, they don't have to matter.

13.

Truth, lies & Christmas in the doghouse

My marriage has been going wrong for a while and last year I had an affair. I have two small children, so I decided that I had to call it off. But now the very thought of sleeping with my husband makes my flesh crawl. Will it ever get any better? My husband doesn't know about the affair.

As Phillip Hodson, a psychotherapist and Fellow of the British Association for Counselling and Psychotherapy, says: 'The price you pay for having an affair is learning to live with the guilt.' And the trouble with your kind of infidelity is that the problems that propelled you into the arms of another are still there now that the liaison has ended.

To compound your discontent, you are now judging your marriage against an idealized relationship that was never subject to the same stresses and strains; it is not a realistic comparison. The day-to-day domestic dust that builds up on the once shiny marriage never has time to settle in an affair. Thanks to maid service and mini bars, half-hour trysts in hotel rooms remain honeymoon-fresh, whereas the greying sheets at home hold no surprises, and you have to wash them afterwards. Guilt will drive a woman to trade high-octane excitement for passionless normality, but it is not an easy trade. Part-time love is a champagne-fuelled fantasy that is exempt from gas bills, trips to the supermarket and cleaning out the guinea pig's cage.

Being desired makes a woman feel fabulous; a combination of lust and anxiety can eat away 5 kg (10 lb) overnight. Ironically, a husband can feel so threatened by his wife's emotional detachment that he will at last begin to pay her the kind of attention that might have stopped her from straying in the first place.

It's a heady cocktail but, ultimately, infidelity is a hopeless trap because, as you are beginning to realize, the demise of the affair creates intense dissatisfaction. It is a rare woman who can switch off feelings for a lover overnight. But she can hardly tell her husband this when he asks her why she seems so depressed.

Instead, she turns her back on him in bed, leaving him in no doubt that whatever is the matter, it is all his fault. Guilt, if not neutralized, can be very corrosive, eating away at the foundations of a relationship until it seems as if the only solution is to be brutally honest.

Invariably, however, the wronged spouse will most likely interpret a retrospective confession as brutal rather than honest, and the relationship will hit the buffers anyway. If your marriage is to have any chance of surviving, you need to find a way of dealing with your guilt so that it does not impede your progress. I doubt that there are many people in whom you can confide, so some individual counselling would be helpful. It would enable you to process your confusion in a neutral environment and help you to work out what has been driving your behaviour so that you could then engage 'honestly' in relationship therapy with your husband.

You can find an accredited relationship counsellor through the British Association for Counselling and Psychotherapy. Counselling is a subjective process and the quality of the help and advice is largely dependent on the skill of the therapist you choose. It is worth noting that studies have shown that integrative behavioural couples therapy has a higher long-term success rate than traditional couples counselling.

Rehabilitation is going to take time and your sex life will improve only when the ghost of your former lover has been exorcized. Remind yourself that you have chosen to stay with your husband for very valid reasons. You've made mistakes, but ultimately you have put your children's needs first, and that is truly commendable.

I have been married for 20 years but there were never sexual fireworks even at the start. My husband is gentle and considerate, but within two years my desire was flagging. Recently I had a passionate snog with another man. Nothing more happened, but it charged me in away that I have rarely experienced. Would this chemistry last, or does it always have a sell-by date of a couple of years?

Sexual desire does wane in all long-term relationships. The rate of 'coital frequency' halves within the first year of marriage and continues to decline the longer a couple has been together, yet married couples still have more sex than any other social group. On average, married people between the ages of 33 and 45 have sex once or twice a week, but only 26 per cent of single men and 22 per cent of single women can make that claim.

Men and women can survive without sex in a relationship, but they usually do so at the expense of basic emotional and physical needs. Sex is enormously beneficial, but as David Goldmeier, of the Jane Wadsworth Sexual Function Clinic, says: 'Once a couple stop having sex, even for a few months, they slip into "non-sexual relationship mode", where it becomes very difficult to initiate sex. They, in effect, become platonic partners in a conspiracy of silence.'

Couples who do not enjoy sex with each other maximize the risk of one or other of them having sex with someone else. It happens everywhere, but Helen Fisher, a biological anthropologist and research professor at Rutgers University, says: 'It is unrealistic to believe that we can evolve to share our partners. If that was possible, polyamory would be huge, but it isn't because we don't share easily.'

Dr Fisher maintains that human beings have evolved three core brain systems for mating and reproduction: lust (the experience you had with your male friend); romantic attraction (flowers, lust and an ego trip); and attachment (the feelings you had, and may still have, for your husband). Love can start with any of these three feelings, in any sequence, and then sex cements the attraction by driving up levels of dopamine and releasing the attachment hormones oxytocin and vasopressin at orgasm. This cocktail has the power to push people over the threshold towards falling in love, which makes it a fabulous and a dangerous experience. As Dr Fisher points out: 'The combination of chemicals it generates means that casual sex isn't always casual.'

Two in five British marriages now end in divorce and Dr Fisher believes that, as a species, we are now moving away from lifelong commitment towards a kind of serial monogamy. Till death do us part, Dr Fisher says, is a hangover from our agrarian ancestors who had a vested interest in marital stability. A farmer who married his daughter to the son of the farmer next door needed to keep that unit intact, but that has changed. As Dr Fisher says: 'You can't divide a cow, but you can divide a ten-dollar bill.'

But enough anthropology; you want to know whether the chemistry you feel would last. Well, 60–67 per cent of second marriages fail and 73–74 per cent of third marriages do, too, so the answer has to be no. It is also true that couples who initiate an affair and do not act decisively to consolidate the relationship within the first few months of meeting are unlikely to do so in the future. You have had a near miss and, before your situation becomes anymore complicated, I think you should tell your husband what has happened.

The truth will serve two important purposes. First, it will diffuse the power of the wonderful fantasy you have created and equate it, realistically, with its equal and opposite potential for destruction. Second, the shock of your revelation will force you and your husband to have a debate about the problems with your sex life. Counselling and sex therapy are obvious next steps, but sometimes the naked honesty that emerges when the truth finally outs is all that it takes for two people to realize how much they have built and achieved together and how miserable they would feel if they threw it all away for an uncertain liaison.

I'm 34 and have been married to my husband for five years – we were together for seven years before that. We have bought a house and aim to start a family this year. The problem is that I have developed a secret crush of staggering proportions on a colleague and it is having a terrible effect on my marriage. I am avoiding sex and we are rowing, too. What can I do to cure myself of my stupidity?

The feelings that you have for your colleague meet the psychiatrist Frank Pittman's definition of a romantic affair – one that happens 'not when you meet somebody wonderful (wonderful people don't screw around with married people) but when you are going through a crisis in your own life'. Stupid crush aside, you describe your married life as close to perfect, but the fact that you have been hijacked by an involuntary infatuation right at the point when you are supposed to be contemplating motherhood is either the world's biggest coincidence or a subconscious attempt to avoid what you presume to be the logical next step in your meticulous life plan.

You are clearly not an irresponsible person. At a time when your peer group were out clubbing every night you and your husband were busy clocking up the mileage on your commitment, announcing your engagement, planning the wedding, saving for a house and working towards the day when you might start a family. The choices you made back then were the ones you felt were right for you at the time. You had good reason to be more concerned with creating future security than playing the field. Perhaps the prospect of starting your own family dredges up anxieties about your own upbringing. Or maybe some part of you regrets the fact that your craving for security denied you the opportunity to experiment sexually and now you realize that once children enter the equation your marriage will be cemented, literally.

Denise Knowles, a Relate counsellor, suggests that you 'explore what it is about your colleague that you find so appealing and see if that gives you any insight into what might be missing from your life'. She also urges you to recognize that even if your biological clock has started ticking 'there is no rule that says you have to have kids now'. You certainly should not contemplate having children if you suspect that you might have an affair. Of 280,000 paternity tests conducted by the American Association of Blood Banks, 30 per cent of the children in the sample were fathered by someone else. Other studies suggest that one child in ten has a different paternity.

Either way, the recent case of 22-year-old Elspeth Chapman, who has been disowned by the man she considers to be her father after a paternity test revealed that his former wife had been lying to him since her birth, is an object lesson in the havoc that such deception can wreak on innocent people.

The first flush of infatuation is a blindingly seductive experience and it can be difficult to maintain any sense of perspective when you have convinced yourself that the attraction you feel for someone else is the cause, rather than a symptom, of your marital dissatisfaction.

In reality, focusing your energy on a crush just allows you to evade the bigger, more painful questions: is the marriage working and do you want to have children with your husband? If thinking through these difficult questions on your own provides no answers, therapy may help. Phillip Hodson, Fellow of the British Association for Counselling and Psychotherapy, suggests that you try to 'neutralize the fantasy you have created by trying to bring it into the realm of reality'.

Think about what would happen if this frisson progressed beyond a crush. Consider the statistical improbability of a new relationship bringing you happiness, marriage and children. And then find a marriage guidance counsellor for yourself and your husband to tackle whatever it is that is really having a terrible effect on your marriage.

For the past four months I have been involved in an opportunistic sexual liaison with a work colleague, which she has just called time on. It was exciting while it lasted and it made going to work more interesting but it didn't actually mean much to me so I am glad it is over. I love my wife and I don't want to do anything to jeopardize my marriage so I have no intention of telling her what has happened but I am concerned that I found it so easy to cheat. Does that mean it will happen again?

A friend of mine once told me that the only way to keep an affair secret is to shoot the person you committed adultery with. It is sound advice. Although Associated Press statistics suggest that 70 per cent of married women and 54 per cent of married men don't know about their spouses extra-marital affairs, no adulterous partner should ever be arrogant enough to presume that his or her own desire to keep an affair secret will be enough to persuade the world to co-operate.

The trouble with infidelity is that whether your wife knows or not doesn't matter. You know. And that changes the energy in your relationship. An illicit affair is such a high-octane experience that it is difficult not to let it spill over into your life. It is also difficult not to spill the beans to a friend or colleague, but once one person knows, there is no guaranteed way of containing the information.

Some people seem to be able to turn a blind eye to a bit on the side, but for the average marriage infidelity is a deal-breaker. Some people will give their spouse a chance, or even a couple, but then it's the red card and the marriage they didn't want to jeopardize is history.

Most divorces are instigated by women and in about 70 per cent of cases, 'unreasonable behaviour' or 'adultery' is the cause. However, those in the know understand that the term 'unreasonable behaviour' is used as a mask when an adulterer does not want his or her infidelity on record. Infidelity is often a symptom of a troubled relationship because people who are happily married don't tend to sleep around. But that is not true of all adulterers, which is why so many are clear that their infidelity is not a marriage exit strategy. So why do people who want to stay married have affairs? As you say, sometimes the opportunity just presents itself and a desire for excitement or experimentation propels the betrayal, but in reality that kind of unconscious behaviour is rare.

Scratch the surface of someone who walks blindly into an affair and you find someone who is desperately looking for a way of avoiding conflict, or intimacy, or you find a person who is immature, or addicted to thrill-seeking, or someone who is so confused about being married that it is easier to transfer responsibility for his or her issues to a third party so that a more complex set of problems is reduced to: 'Should I leave my spouse for my lover? Or not?'

You obviously didn't engage with this woman on an emotional level. However, if you can have extra-marital sex without feeling anything for the person, then yes, you are likely to do it again, unless you address the issues that compelled you this time. It might help to write down what you remember your life being like before the affair. Analyse how you were thinking and then ask yourself honestly, with hindsight, if you would do the same thing again in the same situation. If the answer, genuinely, is no and the experience has made you value your wife more than you did prior to the affair, then don't let guilt destroy that feeling and try to put the past behind you. If, on the other hand, you realize that you are not happy either personally or within your relationship, then you should consider individual therapy, couple counselling or sex therapy. Good luck.

At Christmas, when my wife playfully wrestled with her sister, it turned me on. I told her the truth but she says I'm disgusting. Now I'm in the doghouse.

Christmas. It's a nightmare, isn't it? There is something about the combination of alcohol, inertia and being cooped up with the in-laws that almost guarantees inappropriate behaviour. The combined strain of booze, boredom and being forced to spend time with people you generally try to avoid will split small cracks in any relationship wide open.

Over the festive period, the marriage guidance company Relate receives a 50 per cent surge in the number of calls it receives. Come the new year, the miserable process of paying for a holiday that is primarily geared towards six-year-olds consolidates the gloom – particularly if you didn't enjoy it –

and more couples begin the divorce process in January than in any other month of the year. It is not an excuse but, in different circumstances, I doubt you'd have been so dumb as to say something so crass to your other half. That's not to say you wouldn't have thought it. You probably would have.

Sisters – two sisters wrestling, two sisters getting it on with each other, two sisters competing for the same guy or two sisters getting it on with the same guy at the same time – have always been a favourite male fantasy.

But it is not one that any sensible male would actually share with his wife. This is because, while a fantasy about group sex between your wife and her sister does no one any harm, when aired in public that fantasy has the power to undermine your wife's ability to trust two of the most important people in her life.

As the anthropologist Margaret Mead once said: 'Sisters are probably the most competitive relationship within the family.' And, although your fantasy was to do with both of them, it is likely that your wife has interpreted your comments as an expression of sexual interest in her sister.

That's an unbelievably threatening proposition for her to deal with and, unless you can restore her faith in you, not only will you have damaged your own relationship with her, you may also have damaged her relationship with her sister.

Away from the pressure-cooker environment of giftwrapped Santa Claus boxer shorts and after-dinner port, I'm sure you can see how foolish it was to turn a few minutes' titillation into a legitimate cause for concern. But since you can't take your comment back, the best thing you can do now is to grovel.

Tell her that you are really sorry, that you didn't mean it, that you feel like an idiot, that you are ashamed at having upset her and, most importantly, tell her in no uncertain terms that you are not, and never have been, sexually interested in her sister and vice versa.

The only way for you to resolve this problem is to take personal responsibility for causing it. She probably won't forgive you immediately. You have behaved like a dog so you must expect her to behave like a bitch for a while. Plenty of stroking, petting and ego-massaging will help. SpaceNK bath products, Pierre Marcolini chocolates and Aqua di Parma scented candles are also effective. They are expensive but, when it comes to women, absolution is often directly proportionate to the price a man pays for his penance.

14.

Porn, flakes & cybercheats

My husband of five years masturbates to internet porn. He doesn't seem to fancy me and won't touch me. Is it the end of our physical relationship?

It might be the end of your relationship, period. When a man has a better sexual relationship with an online porn star and his right hand than with his wife, something is seriously wrong. I know, I know, masturbation is normal. And if 'normal' constitutes majority behaviour, so is jacking off in front of internet pornography.

A 2001 study of 7,037 adults in the US found that 75 per cent of respondents admitted masturbating while online – so it's not as if your husband is the only one. And he's got plenty to look at. There are more than 260 million pages of porn online, an increase of 1,800 per cent since 1998.

Things that are popular also become influential, which is a problem, because porn degrades women and that affects how men view women. And how women view themselves.

And how women behave. From toddlers wearing 'porn star in training' T-shirts to the huge growth in demand for breast implants, women have concluded that if they can't beat the porn squad, they might as well join it. If 75 per cent of men are in the study beating off to pneumatic Barbies with a 38 in chest, the only way to get them out of the study is to get a 38 in chest, too.

The wife blames herself for not being as hot as the on-screen dollies, so she 'tries harder'. But he is still not interested in sex with her. And when she eventually calls him on this, he throws his eyes up to Heaven and says 'jeez, it's not like I'm cheating on you'.

The study I mentioned reported that two thirds of those who visit websites with sexual content said that their online activities hadn't affected sexual frequency with their partners. They lied. One in ten of the people seen by Relate blames the internet for his difficulties and two thirds of the 350 divorce lawyers who attended a 2003 meeting of the American Academy of Matrimonial Lawyers said that online porn contributed to more than half the divorce cases, compared to an almost non-existent role ten years earlier.

In the US alone there are 200,000 online porn addicts, 95 per cent of them men. The majority would not have become hooked on porn but the accessibility, anonymity and affordability makes cyberporn a much more dangerous addiction. For the men that get help to overcome their addiction the catalyst is usually a partner discovering his compulsion, so you need to be tough. Tell your husband that he has to choose between you and the online porn stars. You might want to remind him that they don't do ironing, cooking or waiting in for the engineer, or even real sex.

Oh, and neglecting your wife constitutes 'unreasonable behaviour'. Which is grounds for divorce.

I have a long-term partner whom I still love but I have entered into an email flirtation with someone I barely know. We have only met once and I have no intention of meeting him again, but instead we flirt outrageously via email. I do not get this

kind of thrill from my partner. Am I being unfaithful and should I tell him?

Yes you are. And no you shouldn't. Fidelity comes from the latin words 'fides', meaning faith, and 'fidere', meaning to trust. And successful relationships depend on both. Even though the only physical contact you have had so far has been with your keyboard, it is highly unlikely that telling your partner about your e-male would lead to anything other than permanent residency in the dog house with Fido (Latin for faithful dog).

Most online romances are saved by the fact that one party invariably resides in Wisconsin, the other in Bognor Regis, and never the twain shall meet. But the ease with which people can now fulfil their sexual fantasies without leaving (or losing) the comfort of their own home has made the issue of intellectual infidelity infinitely more complicated. Mrs V. Ordinary carries on having domestic intercourse with her husband, but in her head she's being banged senseless by the smooth-typing American who has been charming the pants off her in a chatroom for the past six months.

The fact that you have already met this guy suggests that, unlike most online connections, you could actualize your fantasies by hopping on a bus. This worries me. Assuming that you first met him before your screens steamed up, it's unlikely that another encounter would lead to anything other than a storming sex session because despite the fact that you barely know him, you have already concocted a fantasy of sexual titillation in your head. Potential problems such as basic incompatibility won't penetrate the thick blanket of expectation that currently smothers your common sense because you are projecting an ideal on to a delusion.

In a way, it's completely understandable. Unlike the plod of 'real life' relationships, affairs are a hot frisson of immediate gratification. Illicit sex feeds the ego. And it can temporarily fill the cracks in a tired relationship because when you go home for tea afterwards, you're so tired that a quiet night in watching Corrie is charming and relaxing, as opposed to tedious in the extreme.

But there is a downside. Having your cake and eating it eventually makes you sick.

The pressure of sustaining two relationships and keeping one secret inevitably becomes an enormous strain. And then there's the withdrawal symptoms, the feelings of insecurity and frustration. In the short term this stuff makes you irritable, jumpy and confused. In the long term it can lead to depression, ill health and even a heart attack. People with heart conditions have a statistically higher chance of having a stroke during sex if they are being unfaithful.

Infidelity can make life more interesting, but ultimately it is dangerous, exhausting and terribly complicated, which is why most people avoid it. From what you say, you are not unhappy. You certainly don't want to go through the hassle of splitting up. But the chance of sexual stimulation with someone new has presented itself – so, why not? You remain technically faithful because you restrict yourself to communicating online, but fidelity is clearly less tangible if what goes on in your head can be called into question. Only you can decide if the buzz that you get when you have 'new mail' crosses the boundaries of conventional communication but there's a lot to be said for Catholic guilt when you are trying to make moral choices about right v. wrong. Ultimately, it goes back to 'fidere', which in case you've forgotten, means to trust. Would you trust yourself?

I have discovered that my husband of 25 years has had an online and telephone relationship with another woman. He works away from home and what began as chat soon developed into sending explicit texts and making phone calls

(not sexual, he says). While he is distraught and swears that it will never happen again, I am overwhelmed by the sense of betrayal. How can I rebuild my trust in him?

While your husband may well be telling the truth about the fact that he and another woman exchange sexually explicit texts but prefer to chat about the weather on the phone, I can understand why you might doubt the veracity of his story.

Whenever a person hides an intimate relationship from his partner he or she is being unfaithful. However, a recent survey by *Divorce Magazine* suggests that when it comes to infidelity gender differences apply. Sexual exchanges over the internet do not count as adultery according to 54 per cent of the men in its survey. I suspect that 100 per cent of those men would change their mind if they caught their wives logging on as 'Sexy MILF looking for naughty fun'.

Do not underestimate the impact of your partner's deceit. It can take up to two years to get over infidelity.

Research into the reactions of betrayed spouses shows that they resemble the symptoms of post-traumatic stress disorder – the most severely traumatized are those, like you, who had the greatest trust and were the most unsuspecting. No matter how penitent your husband is, in these early stages, expecting him to make you feel better will only make matters worse. You need to talk to a counsellor or a friend who can listen in a supportive and non-judgmental way. It is crucial that the person offers only comfort and avoids validating knee-jerk reactions because right now you are too emotional to make decisions that are in your best interest.

It sounds as though your husband is prepared to abandon his affair and work at the marriage. That is important because unless both parties are equally committed marriage-guidance counselling is hopeless.

Rebuilding your trust in him will not be easy. First, you will need to identify his motivations because unless the underlying cause is addressed he is likely to do it again.

You also need to be told the whole truth about what happened in the relationship. He may be reluctant to do this for fear of hurting you even more, but concealing the details will leave questions unanswered and that will prevent you moving on. During this process of unravelling it is possible that you will hear some harsh truths about the state of your marriage, but infidelity is not necessarily an indicator that a relationship is troubled.

Unfaithful partners will always argue that they were not getting enough from the marriage but it is often the case that they were not giving enough either.

Your husband does not sound like a philanderer, but the fact that he works away from home has given him the opportunity to stray and often that is all it takes. In the past 15 years the anonymity, disinhibition and accelerated intimacy that internet exchanges allow has created a crisis of 'unintentional' infidelity that has now been fully commercialized.

There are even websites designed for married men and women who want to play away from home. They find each other at the click of a mouse and, unsurprisingly, the number of divorces triggered by online affairs is now 33 per cent and rising.

Several factors influence whether a couple can survive an affair, but the most important one is the quality of their relationship before it, because this determines their level of commitment to repairing things. Good communication is also important, as is a willingness to seek help in the form of individual and couple counselling.

The good news is that couples who survive infidelity often find that they develop a stronger relationship because they are forced to examine what went wrong with their relationship in the first place.

I have just discovered that my boyfriend of ten years has been using online sex chat rooms with a view to meeting up in real life, although my discovery means he hasn't had a chance. He argues that he hasn't been unfaithful since nothing has happened, but I feel that he has been emotionally unfaithful. I feel betrayed and he thinks he hasn't done anything wrong. How can we resolve this?

There is no way that you, singular, can resolve this issue. One of the most galling things about infidelity, whether on- or off line, is that you, the person who feels wronged, do not get to decide whether you want to make things right.

No matter how hurt, humiliated and betrayed you feel, you do not have the power to control the eventual outcome of the situation. Your boyfriend does. He gets to choose whether he is willing to acknowledge that his behaviour is a problem, and if he can be bothered to change it. He may have had only virtual sex to date, but the ACE (anonymity, convenience, escape) model of cybersexual addiction — as defined by Dr Kimberly Young, an acclaimed expert on internet addiction — shows that disinhibition, accelerated intimacy and hypersexual online behaviour are a pretty accurate predictor of real-world transgressions. I suspect you don't know the half of what he has been up to, not that it really matters. Ellen Helsper, research fellow at the Oxford Internet Institute, University of Oxford, says: 'Couples do not make a distinction between online or off line infidelity because the emotions, and the sense of betrayal, are the same.' Helsper recently collaborated with William Dutton and Monica Whitty on an international investigation into the impact of the internet on marital relationships. The results of *Me, My Spouse and the Internet: Meeting, Dating and Marriage in the Digital Age* reveal high levels of agreement between married partners about the unacceptability of online physical and emotional infidelities.

Whitty, who is based at Nottingham Trent University, and is the co-author of *Truth, Lies and Trust on the Internet* and *Cyberspace Romance: The Psychology of Online Relationships*, also says that 'participants who engage in cybersex and erotic talk online are clear that their behaviour constitutes an act of betrayal'.

So I sent her your question.

Whitty describes your boyfriend's behaviour as 'emotional betrayal' and says that his 'plan to meet the person face-to-face makes this transgression even more painful'. Damn right. Happy couples don't hurt each other in this way.

Healthy relationships don't tend to stop at cohabitation either. Long-term relationships have a natural momentum that steers couples towards increased levels of commitment. Whether that commitment evolves as marriage or children or both is immaterial, but the absence of either in a ten-year relationship would ring alarm bells for most people.

It can be really difficult to retain a sense of perspective when you have spent a third of your life with one person, so it may be an idea to share this problem with a close friend or family member who knows you both and can offer you an objective opinion.

Counselling is an option but, again, your boyfriend gets to choose whether he wants to engage. And when a woman feels betrayed it can be incredibly irritating to have to listen to a therapist telling you that your boyfriend's cybersexual encounters are a symptom of underlying problems in your relationship, and that to maximize communication you need to suspend your feelings of betrayal and avoid judgmental language in favour of non-blaming statements such as 'I feel neglected when you stay up all night reading porn-filled emails from strangers'.

Fortunately I have resisted the temptation to trade

journalistic independence for a few letters after my name, so without breaking any codes of practice I can advise you to bin your toxic boyfriend and conserve whatever is left of your self-esteem. It is always difficult to walk away after ten years, but I can tell you from personal experience that hanging around for another five doesn't make it any easier...

15.
Redundancy, gold watches & status anxiety

During sex I am constantly thinking about the mortgage, the kids, the bills and other mundane matters. My husband always seems to be in the moment, how do I get there?

I know how you feel. Life, work, deadlines, shopping, cooking, forgetting to pay the congestion charge, waiting for deliveries that never come, chauffeuring kids around because public transport doesn't work. Unless you find ways of unwinding, the boring, frustrating, thankless rubbish that dulls your day will flood your brain, raise your blood pressure, sabotage your sleep and kill your libido.

Women have different approaches to decompression. Some do yoga; others do chablis. I personally favour half an hour in my Kohler Sok overflow bath. With my husband.

No, I'm not kidding. It cost an obscene amount of money and it had to be lowered in through the ceiling which involved taking up the floor and cutting the joists. But it was worth it. That bath is our 'off' switch. Light the candles, lock the door, and all the mundane matters that would otherwise follow us into bed are left behind.

In theory, having dinner together would do the trick too, but it doesn't (particularly if your kids dine with you).

Cooking, eating, dissecting the day and then clearing up is enjoyable but it is not relaxing and, as the conversation often centres around things that need to be done or issues that need to be resolved, it can aggravate rather than alleviate anxiety. Unwinding in front of the telly doesn't work either. Although it is a physical anaesthetic, it is a mental stimulant and it doesn't encourage a couple to engage with one other so when they go to bed the jump from domesticity to intimacy is just as difficult.

Though statistics still indicate that married couples have more sex than their single counterparts, anyone who has spent more than two years in the same relationship knows that quantity doesn't necessarily indicate quality. The distracted shag before sleep descends might technically qualify as intercourse, but that doesn't mean it is any good.

The male erection translates automatically into sexual desire, but for women arousal is a much slower and more cerebral experience. Because a woman's brain has to be turned on before her body can respond, the nanosecond between a late night erection, ejaculation and unconsciousness doesn't give her enough time to extricate her brain from stacking the dishwasher, let alone encourage her exhausted body into sexual arousal.

Tie the knot and overexposure takes the edge off everything. Sex becomes less of a priority and, if a couple don't seek opportunities to reconnect, the kind of gradual disengagement that you are experiencing occurs. Fortunately, a few simple changes in your evening routine can get things quickly back on track.

What you need to do is make time for some form of mutual wind-down with your husband before going to bed. It doesn't matter what you do as long as it is unstimulating enough to allow you to detach yourself from the day-to-day stuff that will otherwise race round your brain all night. It doesn't need to be a laboured experience; you can simply go for a short walk, or a run, have a drink in the garden, take a bath, cut each other's toenails or read out loud to each other.

Even if you get only 15 minutes together, focusing on you plural provides an opportunity for you to plug into each other again. And because boredom is weirdly conducive to arousal, you'll find that the neutral vacuum you create is frequently filled by better, more intimate, sex.

My husband lost his job three months ago and we haven't had sex since. I find his moping around the house deeply unsexy and that having him under my feet all the time means we argue constantly. He says that he feels emasculated by the redundancy and that my avoiding him in the bedroom doesn't help. But what can I do? I just don't fancy him.

A recession certainly puts 'for richer or poorer' to the test. The economic constraints are tough enough – declining invitations to weddings in France, switching the kids to state education, keeping up with mortgage payments, venturing into Asda for the first time – but the psychological impact of redundancy is worse.

Although most people whinge about having to work for a living, denied the opportunity to do so they quickly realize that much of their identity was tied up in their job. Besides the financial incentives, work also provides structure, routine, social interaction, peer-group validation, and prospects, a ladder to climb. Take that away and the newly unemployed person feels, at best, disoriented, at worst, chronically depressed.

If our lives were more balanced, perhaps unemployment wouldn't make us feel so 'redundant', but most people are, to some degree, defined by the work they do, so unemployment is a huge blow to their self-esteem. In couples where one partner is still employed, financial dependence can tip the balance of power in an unhealthy way. And although couples often complain about not having enough time with each other, as you point out, when two people are at home all day, they can get under each other's feet.

Overexposure can aggravate underlying tensions. From what you say in your letter, his defensivness – 'it's not my fault I was made redundant and all I want is your support' – is matched by your sensitivity – 'it's not my fault you lost your job and I'm scared about the future'. And because neither of you feels listened to or understood, you go round and round in a hugely unsexy cycle of blame and counter-blame, which leaves you feeling so disillusioned that you begin to wonder whether it is only his job that has been lost.

To snap out of this downward spiral, you and your husband need to surrender to the fact that while global economics may be beyond your control, you do have the power to control how you make each other feel and how you help each other cope. This is a time for kindness and white flags, not petty bickering and red rags. It requires a 'glass half full approach' to life because, believe it or not, there are lots of upsides to unemployment.

Many people, me included, have made a conscious decision to view the recession as an opportunity to re-evaluate what is important in life and rediscover non-material values. OK, you and your husband might be cash-poor, but you are time-rich, and that's priceless. If you could get beyond your hostility, the two of you could stay in bed on rainy Monday mornings and make out. And yes, tighter budgets rule out lavish lunches, but lengthy picnics are much more fun anyway. Instead of buying stuff you don't need, why not sell stuff you don't want on eBay? Expensive spas? Who needs them when you can have a bath and a massage with a Jimmyjane afterglow massage candle.

And remember all those promises about getting fit? Well, get those trainers on because exercise has been scientifically proven to increase sexual drive, sexual activity and sexual satisfaction. The psychological benefits of physical exertion include stress relief, increased self-image and self-confidence. And results of a recent study reported that women were more sexually responsive after 20 minutes of vigorous exercise. Like sex, exercise costs nothing and makes you feel great, but while you and your husband are running, hiking, swimming or climbing, I'd ask you to spare a thought for grey-faced employees who could never afford such a luxury.

I've been with my husband for 18 years and we haven't made love or been sexually intimate for more than a year. I have tried talking about it, and instigating romantic evenings, but his response is 'stop hassling me for sex woman'. I still love him but am seeing him less and less as a husband and more of a room-mate with whom I share a bed. Should I give up?

Sex is the tie that binds a couple together, but it can also be the rope they strangle each other with. When one partner feels physically rejected, as you do, it causes real conflict. Research by Elisabeth Burgess, associate professor of sociology at Georgia State University, found that those who are involuntarily celibate frequently experience anger, self-doubt, frustration and depression.

Though problems in the bedroom often reflect problems in the relationship, it could be that your husband's lack of interest may simply reflect financial concerns or fears about redundancy, or he may be trying to ignore erectile difficulties by avoiding sex altogether.

Whatever the cause, shutting you out is not a great solution, but neither is hassling him. You can't nag someone into wanting sex, so your only real option is to try to work out why he doesn't want it anymore.

In their book *He's Just Not Up for It Anymore*, Bob Berkowitz and his wife Susan Yager-Berkowitz surveyed more than 4,000 men and women in sexless marriages across the US to try to understand this problem. In many cases male sexual performance was affected by illness, erectile dysfunction, side-effects of medications, or alcohol or drug dependency, and of course some men were simply in doubt about their marriage. Just 6 per cent of men blamed it on being 'too tired', and 9 per cent said that they didn't have the time.

Boredom was the biggest issue; 68 per cent of men blamed their partner's lack of sexual adventurousness, although as the authors rightly point out, the men failed to acknowledge that they made no novel contribution to their sexual relationships either.

Depressingly, 48 per cent said that they would enjoy sex with other women, just not their wives, and 25 per cent said they preferred to use internet porn for sex because it was less hassle. Many of them (44 per cent) were angry with their wives, feeling that they were constantly nagged and criticized. And 38 per cent said that their wives had gained a substantial amount of weight and they found them less attractive – their own weight was not a consideration.

The survey also revealed that 68 per cent of women did not know why their husbands had gone off sex and were bewildered and hurt by their partner's indifference towards them. Some felt that sex was being withheld as a punishment and 57 per cent said they felt that their husbands were depressed.

You say that you have already tried to talk to your husband about how you feel, but Yager-Berkowitz suggests that you 'make it very clear that it is a problem for you both and listen to his side, which may not be pleasant'.

That's easier said than done. In her study, both genders were guilty of agreeing more with survey statements that shifted responsibility away from themselves and if you have been going around the houses with this for more than a year now I think a neutral third party would help you both to filter difficult information and soften harsh truths.

You can find a sex and relationship therapist through the College of Sexual and Relationship Therapists, the British Association for Counselling and Psychotherapy or Relate. Re-establishing a long-lost sex life involves a great deal of openness and honesty and both of you will have to quit blaming each other, start forgiving and learn to compromise, but 18 years is very much worth fighting for.

My wife of ten years has lost her desire for sex. She will put up with it occasionally, but obviously that is no fun. We have a son, 7, and I don't want to wreck his life by getting a divorce, but I am not ready to give up a normal sex life. I could seek extramarital relationships, but that would make me a cheating husband. My wife has been to counselling and it did not help. What should I do?

You wouldn't be the first man to contemplate cheating on a wife with low sexual desire. In 2001 the genitourinary medicine unit at St Mary's Hospital in London carried out a survey on 100 women patients; 20 had some form of sexual dysfunction; of those, seven had low sexual desire. Six of those seven women had only ever had sex with their long-term partners, but, curiously, five of the seven had sexually transmitted infections.

The team concluded that some women with low sexual desire do not want intercourse but agree to have sex with their regular partner anyway. However, their partners still feel they need a sexual outlet outside the relationship, and, subsequently, they transmit a sexually transmitted infection back to their primary partner.

To state the obvious – unlike male arousal, female sexual desire is not visible. That makes it difficult to measure.

Scientists have carried out many tests using probes to measure lubrication and responses to sexual imagery, but clinical tests ignore the fact that female sexual desire can have less obvious triggers.

Trust, intimacy, the ability to be vulnerable, non-sexual touching, communication and affection are key motivations for female response.

Clearly the last thing that a woman suffering from low sexual desire needs is a metaphorical gun to her head loaded with threats of divorce or extramarital sex. It is also worth clarifying that when it comes to sex, satisfaction should never be confused with frequency. Many couples, particularly those over 40, have sex once a month, or even less frequently, but importantly, when they do get around to it they really enjoy it.

There is a wealth of evidence to support the link between sexual dissatisfaction and unhappy relationships. Several studies have shown that partners' experiences of unresolved conflicts, not feeling loved and emotional distance are associated with lower sexual satisfaction.

Few women will be surprised to learn that other research has shown that marital therapy which focuses on non-sexual relationship issues are likely to result in significant increases in sexual satisfaction.

When people are happy in their relationships, they are happier in bed. Unfortunately, however, it can take a long time for couples to reach this happy conclusion. It takes an average of six years for troubled couples to seek help (Gottman) and by then it is often too late. It sounds to me as though you and your wife could benefit from immediate professional support. It could help you to understand your individual contributions to this situation. It is only when you both take ownership of the problem that the way forward will reveal itself. In the meantime, be kind, and do be mindful that your son is learning from your behaviour.

You say that your wife has been to counselling but you don't say what this is about. If she is unhappy or stressed for reasons unconnected with your relationship, it would still have an impact.

Depression, for example, would certainly explain her lack of interest in sex. Antidepressants, particularly selective serotonin reuptake inhibitors, SSRIs (Prozac, Paxil, Zoloft), can lead to a loss of interest in sex.

If this is a question of sexual function rather than a relatioship problem, I would recommend the Jane Wadsworth Clinic at St Mary's Hospital, which provides an integrated approach to the treatment of sexual function problems for individuals and couples.

16.

Bad sex, porn Barbie & settling for Mr 30 Per Cent

We've been married for 20 years and my husband has stopped bothering with foreplay. Any tips to make pre-penetrational play more exciting?

Pre-penetrational is such a horrible expression. It suggests a swift appetizer of the half-grapefruit variety, rapidly followed by a main course of dried-out greying meat and gravy. It sounds institutional, medical, enormously unappealing and, in all honesty, I can't suggest any way of 'making it more exciting'. I could, I suppose, suggest that you insist on cunnilingus and kissing before progressing to penile stimulation, but quite frankly, foreplay is about so much more than the mechanics of licking and poking.

In fairness to you both, 20 years of marriage doesn't do much for anyone's sex life and the fact that the two of you are still having any at all bodes well. However, when it gets to the point where sex constitutes a brief and infrequent act of intercourse, you are both getting so little out of the exchange that it is probably safe to predict that in another ten years you won't have to worry about pre-penetrative play anyway.

To halt this inexorable slide towards a life of complacent celibacy you need to stop thinking about adding forced play to your already lethargic lovemaking and start getting some real intimacy and connection and creativity back into your sexual relationship.

Because abstinence makes the heart, and various other organs, grow fonder, I think the first thing you both need to do is to stop having sex. Radical maybe. But you need to create some sexual tension and implementing a ban is the easiest way to achieve this. Obviously, you will need to get your husband to agree, and convincing him will mean presenting the concept in a positive and intriguing way.

Don't criticize his performance or whinge about not getting enough foreplay. And don't tell him what you are up to. Just explain that you intend to give your sex life a makeover and that he simply has to trust you and follow your instructions. Men so rarely get the opportunity to surrender themselves to sexual directions that he will probably jump at the chance. And if he doesn't, don't worry. He will understand everything in due course.

To begin, you will need some props: a pen, ten sheets of paper and ten stamped envelopes, five addressed to you and five addressed to him. On the top of each of the first five sheets of paper write one of the following headings: five things I love about you; five things I love about having sex with you; five things I want us to do together before we die; five things I want us to do in bed together; and finally, five things I fantasize about but have never told you. Copy those headings on to the other five sheets of paper and then put each sheet in an envelope.

Take your husband out to dinner (being in a public place heightens the sense of anticipation). During the meal hand him the five envelopes that are addressed to you and ask him to look at what is written on each sheet. Explain to him that you will fill in an identical set of letters and post one to him each week. And ask him to do the same for you. You may want to discuss what you might say to each other. You may not. One thing is for sure, though, if you both make an effort to be honest and imaginative, over the next five weeks not only will you learn something about each other, and create an incredible state of anticipation, you will seduce each other intellectually.

Now that's what I call foreplay.

My husband of 21 years will only have sex in the spoons position and only if I lie still and make no noise. I feel like a blow-up doll. We love each other, but maybe he doesn't see me as a sexual being?

Of all the sexual positions, spoons is the one that requires the least exertion. A man doesn't generally have a great deal of opportunity to thrust, but he can fondle his partner's breasts and play with her clitoris. It is a fantastic position for people recovering from illness or surgery, for those who have bad backs or stiff joints, or who are generally geriatric.

The huge downside to spoons, particularly when it is the only position on offer, is that a man cannot see his partner. Unless, of course, that is an upside. I can see why you are distressed. Your husband chooses to have sex in a position that requires little or no effort on his part. He chooses a position in which he does not have to look at you, and he does not allow you to move or make any noise.

Unless he can come up with a valid explanation, by anyone's standards, his sexual behaviour is completely unacceptable. You say that you love each other but the way he treats you in bed is far from loving. Having said that, if you have never complained to him about the way it makes you feel, he has no way of knowing that you hate it. Only by making your needs known can you get them met, and no one else can do that for you.

The keys to successful relationships are communication,

negotiation and conflict resolution. How do the two of you score on those fronts? If you have a few minutes to spare, visit the Gottman Institute website and go to the relationship quizzes section. Mathematician and psychology professor John Gottman (the man who devised the tests), is renowned for his work on marital stability and divorce prediction, and the tests are designed to help couples evaluate their relationship a bit more objectively. The tests analyse the closeness of your relationship and the strengths and weaknesses in your connection with each other.

Gottman has spent decades studying couples' emotions, physiology, and communication. His basic premise is that respect and affection are essential to all good relationships and that contempt destroys them.

I think you'd probably agree that the sexual interaction between you and your husband is not respectful, is not affectionate, and is leaving you feeling hostile. That's a dangerous place to be if you want your marriage to survive, so you need to change things. Start by asserting yourself and making some demands of your own. Refuse to have sex unless he engages with you, and if he doesn't respond, give him an ultimatum – no sex unless he sees a sex therapist with you.

When we make love it's all wham, bam, thank-you, ma'am. My boyfriend's a lot younger and grew up with internet porn. Is this causing the terrible sex?

The internet is both the best and the worst thing that has happened to the information generation. While young people have unprecedented access to useful information on sex and sexual health they also have unparalleled access to a glut of real filth. Google anything and you will get porn. Buy anything and you will get porn. Email anyone and you will get porn.

Some people argue that this explosion in internet porn has created wildly unrealistic expectations about sex. They say that where magazines like *Playboy* once provided men with a substitute image of the real-life naked woman, internet porn now provides men with an idealized airbrushed version of a woman that never existed in the first place. As a result, young men who have grown up with easy access to hardcore porn in the privacy of their own bedroom can find the transition to real sex somewhat confusing, something of a let-down even. Real women rarely look like the pneumatic Barbies that offer up all orifices and have a vocabulary that is limited to: 'Harder, big boy.' And because porn Barbie doesn't have any sexual needs or make any sexual demands, young men know less than ever about how to satisfy a real sexual partner.

Some say that young women are not helping the situation. Apparently, instead of trying to contradict the bulls**t idea of sex promulgated by the internet, young women are increasingly trying to live up to the hyper-reality that is presented in pornography by having boob jobs and saying yes to anal sex. I say some people because, although it is probably true that internet porn screws up sex for some, many others are intelligent enough to know that watching internet porn and making love to a soft, warm, fleshpot is a bit like the difference between playing Full Spectrum Warrior on Xbox and being on the front line in Iraq. While the onscreen versions of sex and violence are exciting, real-life equivalents can be mind-blowing. Besides, you can't have a post-coital cuddle with a processor.

In terms of technique, the 'wham, bam, thank-you ma'am' is favoured by only three types of man: the premature ejaculator, the selfish tosser and the novice. If you suspect that your young man is one of the first two, then he needs a GP or you need better self-esteem. If he is just a bit green around the gills then you need to do him a favour and show him how to slow down. Don't criticize him. Just use your authority to make him submit. Either play the older wiser girlfriend card, or employ gentle restraints such as a pair of nylons tied around his wrists and ankles, a velvet blindfold and some nice high-quality lubricant, and follow this eight-step guide: 1) Take him to the brink of orgasm as slowly as possible; 2) While you stimulate him, tell him in graphic detail what you want him to do to you when you are finished. Don't dress it up with porno nonsense, real-world foreplay is sexy enough on its own; 3) When you think he is close to climax, stop touching his penis; 4) When the sensation has subsided, start again; 5) Repeat this sequence until he begs you to let him come; 6) Make him promise to follow the instructions he has been given, to the letter; 7) Finish him off; 8) Tell him it's his turn now.

I am in love with a man who shows little emotion. We sleep together but only side by side. I can turn him on but he has never made the first move. He assures me that he is not gay and tells me about passionate encounters with previous girlfriends, which hurts me.

In love, my ass. Honestly. That word is bandied about as a validation for standing by freaks, losers, addicts and abusers all the time… But it's really just an excuse, a wall to hide behind. That you are not responsible for the choices you make if you are 'in love' is nonsense. The truth, and you probably know this deep down, is that people who have a healthy relationship with themselves choose partners who are equipped with a full emotional range, integrity and some kind of moral code.

I don't know how old you are or what your previous relationships have been like, but the fact that you would entertain settling for a man who might be gay, who doesn't want to have sex with you and who taunts you with tales of passionate previous encounters, suggests that you don't have a terribly high opinion of yourself.

If you did, you certainly wouldn't allow yourself to fall in love with someone who offered you so little.

Think about it. You choose your clothes carefully. You think about what hairstyle suits you. You shop around for the right job, the best mortgage, the most suitable property. Why, then, would you plump for a boyfriend who is a cold fish.

Every relationship that we have provides important clues to who and what we are but very few of us choose to process that information. When things go pear shaped it is easier to believe that there is something wrong with our other half because, if they are not the problem, we are.

Blamelessness is an attractive delusion but it is not a terribly helpful one, particularly if you keep making the same mistakes over and over again. I can't count the number of friends who say to me at the end of yet another failed relationship: 'I just seem to be a loser-magnet'; or 'Why can't I just meet a nice guy for once.' They never consider that there might be an element of personal responsibility involved in both the setting up and the sabotaging of these relationships. Though they usually have a point about the men that they bin, or get binned by – nothing is ever one person's fault because choosing to be in the relationship in the first place makes both parties complicit.

The main reason people settle for inappropriate partners is fear of being alone. We suffer from such an endemic fear of singleness that many of us would rather be in a dysfunctional relationship than no relationship at all. I once heard the newspaper columnist and TV presenter Janet Street-Porter discussing the Bridget Jones film *The Edge of Reason*. She said that she felt an affinity with Miss Jones because she remembered what it was like going out every night hoping to meet Mr 60 Per Cent – and then realizing that Mr 30 Per Cent would do.

It's sad because, although being single might not be an ideal state, comparatively, nothing feels lonelier or more miserable than being in a relationship with someone who is one part nice, two parts nasty. On a day-to-day basis you walk on eggshells. You compromise your feelings; you bite your lip; and after weeks, months, or even years of isolation, immobilization, frustration and lack of communication, what do you have to look forward to? The pain of your inevitable and long-overdue break up.

So take a short cut. Get rid of him now while your self-esteem is still intact. Then take a long hard look at your relationship history (who you have gone out with; why it has gone wrong). If you see any recurring patterns, try to figure out why you made those choices, what you might have been acting out, or what you might have been hiding from.

17.

Timetables, tactics
& 'not tonight darling'

My girlfriend and I are both very busy, so she schedules sex into our diaries. I secretly hate this; how can I convince her to be more spontaneous?

Spontaneous sex is something that tends to confine itself to the first six months of any relationship. By the time a couple are familiar enough to break wind in front of each other, their sex life has usually nestled into a corner of the sofa and learnt how to hog the remote control.

Statistics on 'how much' sex people are having tend, therefore, to be reassuring. However, the answers to 'why not?' will be depressingly familiar to any couple close enough to consider full make-up non-essential. A survey by US *Elle* and MSNBC.com that asked readers to give reasons why they hadn't had sex in the last month, came up with the following: 42 per cent of women and 47 per cent of men said they had been too busy or stressed; 34 per cent of women and 38 per cent of men said they went to bed at a different time from their partner; 35 per cent of women and 53 per cent of men said they weren't interested; and 23 per cent of women said that they had such negative body image that they didn't want to get naked.

Despite contraception, Viagra and the XXX channel, research shows that women have less sex now than in the 1950s. Recently the Kinsey Institute carried out a survey of 853 women aged 20 to 65 and found that just over 40 per cent who lived with their partners had sex two to three times a week. However, among married women this dropped to 33 per cent. The report puts this down to the fact that '50 years ago few women had jobs, most homes had no televisions and common activities, such as going to the gym, simply did not exist'. Dr John Bancroft, of the Kinsey Institute, says that 'we live in an age where there is little unfilled leisure time' and 'sex used to fill that gap'.

It is true that couples who are too busy or knackered to care about the deleterious effects of falling below national averages for coital frequency almost all notice an upswing in sexual activity on holiday. However, in the same way that the sight of love handles bulging over your bikini briefs is rarely distressing enough to turn you off your tapas, the faintly awkward pressing of slightly over-familiar flesh creates a sexual Post-it Note. But this mental note to have sex with each other is normally long gone by the time the flight home has landed.

The less sex you have with a long-term partner, the less you are inclined to have sex with your long-term partner. Period. So although your girlfriend's scheduling might seem clinical to you, it deserves credit. As you say yourself, you are both busy people. And busy doesn't make for spontaneous. That your girlfriend refuses to allow your commitments to overwhelm such a vulnerable aspect of your relationship shows real commitment and, to be frank, I doubt she would have instigated this system if she felt that you could be relied on to keep sex on the agenda. So instead of undermining her efforts and asking her to be more spontaneous, why don't you try being more spontaneous.

Surprise her with sex when, where, or how she least

expects it. Join her in the shower at 6 a.m. before she leaves for work. Take her to lunch in a hotel and book a room so that you can make out between courses. Lay a duvet in front of the fire/fan, cover it with rose petals and make love when she gets home from work.

Wake her in the middle of the night and... on second thoughts, don't wake her.

After a day like that she deserves her sleep.

My friend announced the other night that she and her husband have been having sex every day to improve their love life. She said that they had got out of the habit and that this new approach was making a real difference to their relationship. According to her, it's now something she makes sure she does at night, like brushing her teeth. Do you think this would work for myself and my partner? We have been together eight years and have definitely got out of the habit.

There are a gazillion reasons why sex tails off in all long-term relationships but ultimately, most boil down to life being exhausting – and you've had sex with each other quite a lot before, so after a tough day its easier to opt for an activity that requires the gentle stimulation of an index finger on a remote control over one that involves the exertion of every single muscle in two tired bodies.

The apathy is a mutual conspiracy at first. You feel safe enough with each other to let it all hang out. He's seen your greying bras and you've seen his toenail clippings. It's a different, shabbier, kind of intimacy, and it's fine for a time – but little by little the lack of investment begins to devalue your relationship. It's a very subtle shift, one which the journalist Tim Scott wrote about rather movingly. He describes the absence of sex in his marriage as 'a powerful yet subtle foe', adding: 'It quietly corrodes the most important parts of a relationship – trust, intimacy, passion, respect – and that least analyzed of all attributes, fanciability. If left untreated, the lack of sex can even destroy love. I am convinced many people split up because they forget to make love to each other, and love – along with the feel-good chemical, dopamine, that sex generates – dries up.'

Scott and his wife got their relationship back on track by making a pact to have sex every day, whether they felt like it or not. They weren't alone. Two books have documented the ups and downs of two couples who had made a commitment to have sex with each other for 365 and 101 days respectively. Charla Muller's *365 Nights: A Memoir of Intimacy* and Douglas Brown's *Just Do It* caused a stir when published in the US, but they received a more lukewarm reception here in the UK. It wasn't only media cynicism. British sex therapists and counsellors were universally snotty about the ideas in the books, denouncing them as 'passive aggressive, prescriptive, regressive and pressurising'. Even though both couples were adamant that their relationships had improved immeasurably and on a multitude of levels, the experts warned that a commitment to daily sex might be a way of imposing unwanted sex on an unwilling partner – fair enough – or that scheduling sex takes away spontaneity. What spontaneity? As you and a million other couples struggling with sexual ennui know, the chances of both halves of a relationship ever being 'spontaneously' in the right place, at the right time, and in the right mood, are pretty slim.

I can't guarantee whether sex every day would work for you and your partner because there may be underlying issues that I don't know about, but if you are both up for the challenge, just go for it. Though working at sex might feel like a contradiction, if you are not happy with your sexual relationship, you need to force change. Instead of waiting for some seismic shift to propel you both back into each other's arms, you need to be proactive, to take steps towards each other. And of course the great thing about a pact to have daily, or even weekly, sex is that it necessitates a) talking about the need for more sex in your relationship, b) agreeing on strategies to enable you to have more sex and c) finding the time to do it. Those three things alone will improve any sexual relationship.

I'm getting married this summer but sex with my fiancée has become dull and infrequent. Will it all be downhill with her from now on?

It could get worse. Right now you are having infrequent sex. By August, you may be having infrequent conversations. Planning a wedding is rarely an aphrodisiac. Quite the opposite, in fact. The angst and anticipation involved in a walk up the aisle can wreak havoc on any relationship.

Look back over the past year and try to work out whether the decline in your sex life corresponds with your decision to tie the knot. If you feel that anxiety about the relationship or apprehension about the wedding could have distanced you from each other, you need to try to communicate those fears to each other. It is natural to have doubts about a commitment as big as marriage, but it can be really difficult to discuss them with each other. Neither of you wants to undermine your commitment, and admitting to nerves might set off alarm bells. However, emotions have a way of manifesting themselves and, if you are worried about any aspect of your capacity to live happily ever after, it is better to get things out in the open sooner, rather than later.

If the wedding isn't the trigger and you have been living with each other for some time, then you may just be suffering from common-or-garden over-familiarity. The Office of National Statistics indicates that 76 per cent of couples cohabit before they get married. This is a good thing because it means that couples are fully informed about all aspects of each other's behaviour if they choose to marry. And it is a bad thing for precisely the same reason.

Overexposure highlights previously unnoticed imperfections. Charming little quirks run the risk of becoming irritating. And sex, once so urgent and mercurial, becomes less frequent and less highly pitched. This is not necessarily negative.

Keeping up the sexual athletics that occur in the first six months of meeting would be exhausting. In a long-term relationship sex has to move to a lower, more sustainable level of intensity or no one would get anything done.

If you and your girlfriend have been together for aeons, your relationship has probably moved into the plateau phase. But if this is the case, you should also experience occasional upswings in the frequency and intensity of your sexual relations. For example, when you proposed and your girlfriend accepted, I would be surprised if you didn't celebrate with a love-in. And as Mr and Mrs Newlywed you can expect to have a lot of sex on your honeymoon. A nice hotel room, Mai Tais by the pool, hot sun and a greater degree of nakedness do wonders for an ailing libido. Sex may be more intermittent when you get back to real life, but you can expect subsequent upturns when you move house, have a fight, make up, change jobs, have a baby, visit parents, get promoted, drunk, fired, lose weight, or go on holiday. So it's not downhill all the way.

Feast or famine, sex in a long-term relationship is not perfect, but it works, so I really wouldn't worry about quantity. Quality is different. You use the word 'dull' in your letter and that bothers me because if you don't like what happens when you make love, and you haven't been able to improve things in the time that you have been together, you need to question whether you and your fiancée are sexually compatible. If the honest answer is no, I would advise you to think carefully before getting married. However traumatic calling off a wedding seems, it is a piece of cake compared with divorce.

My once sexually adventurous wife of over ten years now utterly rejects my advances. She will not say why. What on earth should I do?

Make sure that you've got cable and take up golf? If you are in this marriage for the long haul, brace yourself for a period of celibacy. The female libido is as stubborn as a mule and if your wife says she doesn't want any, she doesn't want any. And don't bother asking her why. She probably doesn't know.

Cynics argue that women are a biological conspiracy designed to trick men into dating, mating and procreating; at which point they immediately lose all interest in sex, lingerie and the size of their ass. But the common and well-documented decline in the female libido in a long-term relationship is more likely to be a symptom of accumulated fatigue brought on by a mundane combination of work, kids, domestic responsibility, financial concerns and snoring.

Marriage is notoriously bad for relationships. Continued overexposure invariably leads to laziness, disinterest, feeling taken for granted, communication difficulties and unresolved arguments. The drip-drip-drip of gradually decreasing sensitivity towards each other is such an effective passion-killer that it has a negative effect on sex drive in pretty much every marriage at some point. But, unlike tangible offences such as infidelity, we are not equipped to analyse or resolve amorphous-ennui or non-specific bickering, which is why your wife can't articulate the combination of frustrations that have led to her sexual rejection of you.

The best thing you can do is to back off and leave her with it. Because women are, by nature, rather contrary, dignified indifference will arouse her curiosity more effectively than nagging, stonewalling and obvious ultimatums such as: 'If you won't, someone else will.' An altruistic approach will make her feel guilty, a vulnerability you can capitalize on by using your period of celibacy as an opportunity to invest in the nonsexual aspects of your relationship with her.

Random acts of affection are the glue that hold a marriage together and although she would probably never admit it, your wife loves it when you do little things that show you care. When did you last take her picture, for example? Or run her a bath? Have you asked her opinion on anything that wasn't directly related to your domestic life recently? Can you remember the last time you took her away for the weekend? Or sat up drinking wine and talking until the early hours of the morning.

For ordinary loss of desire, strategic benevolence can't fail, but sexual issues often mask more serious underlying conflicts and these can be more difficult to fix than minor domestic problems. When you struggle to keep the house clean, you get a cleaner. When you need help with childcare, you get a nanny. But, when your wife won't put out, you don't pay for sex. No. Unfortunately, when kindness and consideration fail to pay dividends you get to hire someone to listen to her telling you what a lousy husband you have been. And then you keep paying them so that they will listen to you getting a few things off your chest. And by the time you are done, both of you are usually so mad at the person you have paid to listen that your adrenalin levels go through the roof and you shag each other's brains out. It's an expensive route back to the marital bed, but it's cheaper than divorce.

**I am 65 and my wife is an attractive woman of 49.
Unfortunately she seems to feel that she is past the age at
which sex is a regular part of marriage. How can I convince
her that it is perfectly normal for a woman of her age to
continue to enjoy an ongoing love life?**

Life becomes inversely more difficult as women age, and
at 49 everything seems to happen at once. Stroppy teens,
elderly parents, rising living costs, declining income,
expanding waistline, shrinking self-esteem. And, oh, I nearly
forgot... menopause.

The average age at which peri-menopause begins is 47, so
your wife is already on the hormonal rollercoaster that marks
the cessation of egg production. While some (Japanese)
women breeze through the menopause, those who discover
the joys of scrambled tofu and soya smoothies in our forties
are still destined to suffer from hot flushes, nightsweats,
palpitations, migraines, mood swings, poor concentration,
disrupted sleep and general irritability. The menopause is
not a sexy moment in a woman's life anyway, but the fact that
one-third of women also experience vaginal dryness, itching,
discomfort, painful sex and/or decreased libido means that
sex is low down on the list of priorities.

Fortunately, it's a finite period in a woman's life, although
when a woman emerges from the menopause she then has to
deal with empty-nest syndrome, possible bereavement and,
because she has been such a bitch for the past three years, a
potentially broken marriage. No wonder middle-aged
women get depressed. Twice as many women suffer from
depression as men and for most of them it comes on at
peri-menopause, but unfortunately one of the side effects
of the treatment – SSRI antidepressants – is loss of libido,
so depressed middle-aged women really are stuck between a
rock and a hard place.

The point that I'm trying to make is that your wife doesn't

think she is past it, she just doesn't feel like it. Stressed-out people of any age and any gender rarely do. Having nine million things to do/worry about/organize/pay kills sexual desire stone dead, but once the stress has passed, life starts to stir in the remains of a woman's libido. For middle-aged women, feeling better physically is crucial.

Your wife should see her GP to have her oestrogen levels measured. Her doctor will be able to suggest a range of oestrogen replacement therapies if appropriate, and if you are not already using lubricant, now is the time to start.

Dietary changes may help, and exercise is hugely important. During exercise the body produces endorphins, which act on the brain to block pain and create feelings of exhilaration, happiness and calmness. Exercise also improves circulation and the increase in blood flow benefits the health of the pelvis and the vagina and improves sexual function.

While there is no magic bullet to make a peri-menopausal woman who doesn't want sex suddenly decide that she is up for it, there is growing evidence that sexual difficulties in midlife tend to stem more from stress or dissatisfying marital relationships than from hormonal changes.

Opening up honest lines of communication is vital because there may be issues bothering your wife that she doesn't feel she can talk to you about. She may be struggling with the 16-year age difference between you, for example. After all, she will still be under 60 when you are 75 and she may be worrying about what the future holds for her.

She may also be struggling with her self-esteem and body image. All women find the ageing process challenging but it can be even more difficult for women who have been defined by their looks. You describe your wife as attractive and, relative to your maturity, her youth must once have been a large part of her identity. However, big age gaps have a tendency to shrink as people grow older together.

There are far greater social and intellectual differences

between a woman of 24 and a man of 40, for example, than there are between a woman of 49 and a man of 65, so while you will always be, as Groucho Marx once said, 'as young as the woman you feel', the reverse may be coming true for your wife.

These issues are tremendously complex and will require great sensitivity on both your parts, but it is worth remembering that a woman who does not respond physically to sexual intimacy will often respond sexually to emotional intimacy. Tenderness, romance, understanding, affection, laughter, creativity and commitment have always been the most effective form of foreplay, and the good news for you is that within two to four years this will all be over.

18.

I do, we don't & sex with the ex

I am due to marry a wonderful man, but he doesn't turn me on. He gives me so much and I know we all have to compromise on some things, but am I doing us both a disservice?

If you are set to marry this man, you have obviously been with him for some time and the relationship isn't going to change once you have a ring on your finger. The concerns you have now will still be there after the honeymoon, so it is important to address them before you make a commitment. Failing to do so would be the real disservice.

Sex might seem like the weak point in your relationship but, as the sexual psychotherapist Paula Hall says: 'It doesn't matter if he doesn't turn you on, as long as he doesn't turn you off. Ultimately, if your relationship is going to last you've got to learn to stoke your own flame and no one can do that for you.'

If there was a strong sexual chemistry between you when you first met, then the fact that he doesn't arouse you now might suggest that you have deeper concerns with the relationship. Sex is one of the first elements to deteriorate when things are going wrong. It is an emotional withdrawal that plays out as a physical withdrawal so, for example, if you are harbouring anger or resentment that you don't feel able to express, those suppressed emotions might manifest as sexual disinterest.

You say your fiancé 'gives' you so much, but as Susan Piver, the author of *The Hard Questions: 100 Essential Questions to Ask Before You Say "I Do"*, says: 'Loving someone and loving your life together are different'. It is also possible that your fear of making the wrong decision is sabotaging your ability to make any decision at all. Marriage is a leap of faith and that can be paralysing for people who are used to being able to control every aspect of their lives.

It's a big commitment; there are no guarantees that it will work out, and that element of risk can be so unsettling that sometimes it just seems easier not to go there.

You want things to be perfect, but how many other relationships do you expect that much of? Is your boss perfect? Are your family perfect? How about your friends? You are not perfect. Nor is your future husband. Your marriage won't be perfect either, but if it's what you both choose, then it'll be good enough.

There is no easy answer to your dilemma, but there are ways that you can clarify how you feel. Sit down with a pen and paper. Make a note of all the things that are positive and negative about the relationship and see which list is longer. Talk your fears over with a neutral third party. Although Relate is best-known for couple counselling it also offers a telephone advice service that might help you. Relate also runs workshops for couples who are making 'big' decisions about their relationship such as moving in together, or getting married.

My second marriage isn't going well and I flirt with my first wife when we meet to discuss our kids. I have the urge to turn the clock back – is this normal?

Lots of people who have been through a divorce look back and wonder whether they did the right thing. They ask whether they could have behaved better or made more of an effort to sort things out. In many cases, if the couple had sought help as soon as they felt their relationship was going wrong, they probably could have avoided divorce. Relate says that most of the couples it sees have endured seven years of fighting before seeking help.

Unfortunately, by the time a couple make a decision to get help, one or both parties has often given up on the relationship. It's a tragedy because anyone who has ever been through a divorce understands how hellish it is. In the heat of the moment, when all you can think about is the freedom that a decree absolute will bring, you can kid yourself that that piece of paper draws a line under the past.

It doesn't.

Even couples who don't have children are surprised at how long it takes to move on from a marriage. Throw kids into the equation and it becomes virtually impossible.

The logistics of kids moving between houses, split Christmases and alternate birthdays involve negotiation and planning, and that can be a tall order for two people who have been locked in conflict for years. Research has shown that children from divorced parents fare better if parental conflict is contained, if they have economic and emotional stability, if they maintain a close relationship with both parents, and if they have a say in shaping access arrangements. Most divorced parents will do their best to deliver some, if not all, of that, but in return their children are expected to adjust to new relationships over which they have no control.

Four weddings out of every ten in the UK are second marriages, but at least 60 per cent of these end in divorce. Nobody knows what the cumulative impact of exposure to successive divorces will have on children, but there is no

I DO, WE DON'T & SEX WITH THE EX

doubt that those who fare best will be the ones whose parents continue to put their needs first. You owe it to your children to make the effort to maintain what hard-earned stability they now have in their lives, but your current behaviour displays a casual attitude to their feelings. They were hauled across the coals during your divorce and they have only just established a reasonable relationship with your second wife, yet you are irresponsible enough to consider reversing all this upheaval.

Christine Northam, a Relate counsellor, would describe someone like you as having an 'attachment problem'. She'd say that you 'feel the grass is always greener'.

I'd say that you need a good slap. To escape the failure of your second marriage by seeking solace with your previous wife suggests such an enormous lack of integrity that it is hard to see how you could have persuaded one woman to marry you, let alone two. My advice is to do the right thing, for once. If you can figure out why you screwed up your first marriage, you might have a chance of salvaging your second. Being able to admit that you have a problem is half the solution and, as Northam says: 'Most people say they know themselves better after counselling and feel it has been a chance to grow.' Grow up, I'd say.

My husband and I are getting divorced. He had an affair five years ago and, despite counselling, our relationship has never recovered. Six months ago we split and he moved out. However, when he comes over to see our two kids we always end up fighting, but then, confusingly, we also end up having the most incredible sex. This has been happening since he moved out. Should we be getting divorced?

The end of a marriage is a lonely, painful experience and it is human nature to take whatever comfort you can along the way. However, unless you or your husband are completely sexually opportunistic, the behaviour you describe suggests real emotional confusion about what you are about to do.

Susanna Abse, a psychotherapist and the director of the Tavistock Centre for Couple Relationships, wonders 'if this pattern of fighting and then getting close is an old one, possibly based on shared fears of either getting too close or getting too distant'. She also suggests that 'your husband's affair and being separated means that those fears are being played out at a much more intense pitch than before'.

Since fear heightens arousal, that would, I suppose, explain the great sex. In 1974, the psychologists Donald G. Dutton and Arthur P. Aron conducted 'the shaky bridge' experiment, which established that when a female approached men and asked them to fill in a questionnaire on a rickety bridge swaying 70 m (230 ft) over a river, they provided much more sexualized content than a control group on a stable bridge over a 3 m (10 ft) drop. Similarly, people are more responsive to sexual come-ons after riding rollercoasters.

While channelling strong emotion into sexual attraction may provide a form of relief for you both, it is a destabilizing way of alleviating tension. Your children must wonder why daddy sleeps over and you must question why you can have great sex, yet you can't have a relationship.

You say that you have already tried counselling, but I suspect that you were too bitter about his affair to really engage in the repair process. Chances are you were having problems before he cheated, but according to the Gottman Institute, the average couple waits six years before seeking help for marital difficulties. The likelihood is that by the time you got to counselling the focus was on his infidelity and not on the issues that may have triggered it.

It is often easier to blame a partner's infidelity, or a generic cause, such as lack of 'communication', than it is to admit individual responsibility for the failure of the marriage, and unfortunately, once divorce is on the table, it has a tendency to create its own momentum. It is seen as the solution, the end of all the problems, but really, it is only the beginning.

As any divorcée will tell you, it is only after the dust has settled that the loneliness, the angst and the inconvenience hit home. Like most decent parents, you will make your children's well-being the priority, so you will bite your lip while you make a U-turn to collect their forgotten homework. If you are really lucky, you will meet someone else and it will be great. Every other weekend.

But then you'll find yourself facing the unenviable task of explaining why he is sleeping on daddy's side of the bed. And it's not just hard for women. Australian research into the effects of marital separation on men found that they still reported strong feelings of anger at having been 'left' by their ex-spouses ten years after their divorce.

Clearly there is good cause for many divorces, particularly for children living in high-conflict, abusive or addictive households. However, in a recent US report, 'Does divorce make people happy?', 86 per cent of couples who had contemplated divorce but stayed together described themselves as considerably happier five years later.

Though it takes a brave, mature and forgiving adult to raise the white flag in the middle of divorce negotiations, the alternative is a bit like drinking poison and hoping that your husband will die. So be brave.

After 27 years of marriage I am getting divorced. I have never made love to anyone other than my wife and, at 49, although I am excited, I am also filled with trepidation. Can you tell me what I should expect?

Realistically? Legal bills, several trips to Ikea and a crash course in microwave meals for one. I don't want to rain on your parade, but a decree absolute doesn't guarantee dancing girls with jiggling breasts and although divorce probably feels like a long overdue liberation right now, it is worth bearing in mind that grass tends to look greener from a distance.

From the confines of your miserable relationship, nothing seems worse than the thought of another evening sitting in front of the telly, eating dinner off your lap, with a partner you have nothing in common with. Until you spend the fifth evening in a row, sitting in front of the telly, eating dinner off your lap – alone. The thing is, even when you absolutely bloody hate each other, and your kids are gone and you've been living separate lives for donkeys' years, there is something indescribably unsettling about saying goodbye to the person that you have been blaming all your unhappiness on since your honeymoon.

The fall guy is gone. And that leaves only you. And you are still unhappy. Which makes you responsible. Ouch.

So, when the divorce is done and dusted, and you are sitting alone in your (smaller) room, what can you expect? Well, you'll have plenty of time to contemplate how much freedom and loneliness can have in common.

Initially, you will probably question whether you have done the right thing but, eventually, you will berate yourself for not getting out of your marriage ten years earlier. At some point, though never as quickly as you would like, you will meet a new lover and then you can expect to feel very insecure. Because you have had only one sexual partner in your life you have nothing with which to compare your lovemaking skills, no gauge by which to measure whether what you have been doing for the past 27 years even counts as sex. So you'll be nervous. And since nervousness is bad for erections, you may find that despite high levels of desire, you will fail to perform.

Don't get all shirty – you asked what you could expect and I'm telling you when you next have sex, be prepared for the possibility that your pecker might let you down. It's not a big deal and, if the woman is nice to you and you can relax, the situation will rectify itself quickly. But I mention it because if you encounter impotence with the wrong woman, and you are not aware that it often happens when a man is anxious, you may get stuck in a cycle where anticipating sexual failure makes it happen all the time.

The good news is that unlike your ex-wife, you shouldn't be short of sexual partners. Though you probably feel a bit long in the tooth for dating, your age actually gives you a demographic advantage. There are far more single women than men over 40 so you'll probably have a lot of fun. In fact, I suspect that you will spend the next five to ten years cramming in all the sexual experiences you missed out on by marrying the first girl you clapped eyes on. Being older means that you'll have to deal with more emotional baggage and you'll have to use condoms and pretend to like other men's children, but other stuff will be the same – love, sex, two-timing, getting caught, being bad-mouthed and binned, and starting again. It's all part of life's rich and exhausting tapestry, the one you fantasized about when you were shuffling around the marital home trying to avoid your wife.

And when the fantasy becomes tiresome, when you have tested and tasted too much, what can you expect? I predict that you will find yourself craving stability, normality and constant companionship. Oh, and someone to eat dinner with, off your laps, in front of the telly.

I have recently divorced my wife of 12 years but have slept with her since our separation. The sex is much better now than when we were together. Why?

Why is the sex between you better now? Well, in no particular order: because she isn't angry that you've left your dirty laundry on the bathroom floor any more; because you haven't called to say you'll be home late for the fourth night in a row; because she goes to salsa lessons instead of cooking you dinner; because you don't nag her about the credit card bill; because she hasn't invited her mother to stay; because she is under no obligation to have sex with you – but she is still willing; because you are flattered that you can still get her to; because it pours a temporary balm over the hurt that you have felt – and the hurt that you have caused; because you can get up and leave and not have to explain where you will be, what you will be doing or who you will be with for the next 12 hours...

Need I go on?

In an ideal world, both parties would emerge from the traumatic process of divorce armed with a greater understanding of what it takes to make and break a marriage. They would learn from their experiences and move on, determined not to make the same mistakes again. But it's not an ideal world and, unfortunately, more couples than would care to admit it find that despite the bickering, the resentment and the legal shenanigans, when divorce delivers the emotional, financial and custodial settlement that they couldn't achieve during their marriage, the sense of relief has a negative effect on their critical faculties.

Cutting the ties that bound them together inadvertently releases the ropes that they were strangling each other with and, as if by magic, the relationship stops hurting. This leads to a state of temporary romantic delusion. Resolution erases the painful past and instead of interpreting the relief they feel as a validation of their decision to divorce, the couple allow this temporary comfort to turn a wall into a door. The motivation can be fear, curiosity, insecurity or arrogance but the result is generally the same. The recently divorced couple embrace their new-found numbness between the sheets.

Very few men and women who come out of a marriage do so with the intention of staying single but, for a newly divorced person, the prospect of never meeting anyone else or embarking on the wrong new relationship is intimidating. Many couples find it easier to opt for a no-strings relationship with the person who previously tied them up in knots rather than to face the great unknown. Even people who have moved on to a new relationship can find themselves idealizing the prospect of sex with their ex. It is human nature to hanker after that which is unattainable and, when a man or woman realizes that the partner they have rejected appears to be attracting attention from other prospective partners, the green-eyed monster rears its head. For these people, persuading the ex to have sex is a thinly disguised attempt to sabotage their previous partner's efforts to move on and form new relationships.

None of this behaviour is particularly healthy. Besides the fact that it jeopardizes new relationships, it leaves the participants feeling soiled and confused, not to mention what it does to children, if there are any. You and your ex can kid yourself that it is only sex, but there is always an emotional element to intimacy so, sooner or later, this is bound to end in tears.

But at least then you'll be able to split up without the cost of a lawyer.

19.

Dysfunction, denial & too much of a good thing

Over the last year I have lost sensation at the point of orgasm. As an otherwise fit and healthy 46-year-old man, this is disappointing. My doctor says it's psychological, but I doubt this.

There was a time when we all trusted doctors unquestioningly but like you, one in four patients now don't trust their doctor's advice (according to a recent Johns Hopkins study). It's hardly surprising when you consider that the average consultation lasts just eight minutes and treatments are often determined by price rather than effectiveness. Not that long ago doctors were the only source of advice about medical problems, but the internet has demystified medicine to a great extent. A recent survey by Opinion Research Corporation established that 60 per cent of people in the US had looked for some type of medical information on the internet. Google, the most popular search engine on the web, is used for medical enquiries so often that the company set up Google Health, a subsite where people can store and manage their health information and gain access to more than three billion medical articles. It's a nightmare for doctors who whinge incessantly about people Googling their headache and turning up at the surgery professing to have a brain tumor, but 60 per cent of doctors also use the internet to help them diagnose difficult conditions. Dr Hangwi Tang, from the Princess Alexandra Hospital in Brisbane, recently researched the accuracy of Google as a diagnostic tool. His study, which was published in the *British Medical Journal*, found that in 15 out of 26 cases, the search engine was able to accurately identify a condition based on three to five specific search terms.

Using the correct search terms is the key. For example in your case, it takes a while to get from 'Loss of sensation at the point of orgasm' to the correct terminology, which is 'ejaculatory anhedonia.' But once you get there, you've can choose from 11,700 pages of information on the condition. Most of them say the same thing. Namely, that loss of sensation at the point of orgasm may be caused by one or more of the following: hyperprolactinaemia – abnormally high levels of prolactin in the blood; hypoactive sexual desire disorder (inhibited sexual desire); low levels of testosterone; spinal cord injury; use (or previous use) of SSRI antidepressants; drug addiction; fatigue or physical illness. Presumably, you'll be able to rule out one or more of these causes straight away, and then you'll need to go back to your doctor, armed with your research and ask him to run some blood tests and refer you to a urologist. It is vital that any underlying physical problems are taken seriously and investigated fully, although there is, obviously, a possibility that your doctors initial diagnosis may prove to be correct.

Some psychologists believe that loss of sensation at the point of orgasm is a kind of penile anaesthesia brought on by living life in the fast lane or suppressed hostility towards a partner. In his book *Thrilled to Death: How the Endless Pursuit of Pleasure is Leaving Us Numb*, Dr Archibald D. Hart, a psychologist and professor at the Fuller Theological Seminary in Pasadena, suggests that we are stuck on a 'hedonic treadmill'; where our addiction to excitement and entertainment are over-stimulating the 'pleasure center' in our brain, thereby diminishing our capacity to experience enjoyment. He blames masturbation, porn, coke, booze, stress, money, consumerism and says 'Our continuous pursuit of high stimulation is snuffing out our ability to experience pleasure'. Hey, you didn't happen to work for Lehman Brothers did you?

My wife and I are 43 and were both virgins until we married at 29. Since then, we have found that my wife has vaginismus and have never had successful intercourse as she finds it painful. We don't want to accept this, despite it being too late to have children.

Not exactly Speedy Gonzales, are you? It takes you 30 years to get your first date, another decade to discover that she's never going to put out for you and, by that time, whoops, you've forgotten to have children. What kind of a half-assed approach to life is that? If you don't want to accept your wife's condition why haven't you done anything to sort it out? It's not as if you haven't had the time.

Fourteen years is definitely what you'd call a window in your diary. That you and your wife have demonstrated such fantastic apathy towards your sex life suggests active avoidance as opposed to negligence. It makes me believe that you have been complicit in allowing your wife's vaginismus to disable the possibility of intercourse. There are umpteen treatments for vaginismus available to those who can be bothered to seek them out and any functional couple would have done so years ago. That you have chosen not to makes me think that your wife's problem is very much your problem, too.

If, as you say, you are unwilling to accept the current

situation, the first thing you need to do is book a 'double' appointment with your GP. Appointments are generally only ten minutes long and it can take a while to get to the bottom of sexual problems.

Alternatively, contact a family planning clinic. Most are staffed by doctors who are trained in psychosexual matters and they are particularly good with problems such as vaginismus. Genitourinary medicine (GUM) clinics are also very helpful on sexual issues. Some have clinics with specialists who are trained in psychosexual counselling as well as sex therapy. Your other option is to contact Relate. Although the organization is primarily known for marriage guidance, a number of its counsellors have specific psychosexual training.

Your GP may refer your wife to a consultant at the Institute of Psychosexual Medicine. This is a private organization of doctors though some will see patients without a GP's referral. You could also contact the College of Sexual and Relationship Therapists.

When treated by a specialist in sex therapy, success rates for vaginismus are high. Treatment combines an extensive therapy programme of education, counselling and behavioural exercises. The educational treatment covers sexual anatomy, physiology and the sexual response cycle, and debunks common myths about sex, information which, I suspect, will be very beneficial to both of you.

Your wife will be required to do pelvic floor exercises to improve her voluntary muscle control. She will also have to do vaginal dilation exercises using plastic dilators in graduated sizes. All the exercises are done under the supervision of a sex therapist and treatment involves you too, because intimate contact is gradually introduced between the two of you and this ultimately results in supervised sexual intercourse. Though that sounds a bit terrifying, you will not be the first couple to experience this and you won't be the last. The therapists who treat you will have seen it all before and their only aim will be to help you to help yourself.

I do hope you will both be brave enough to sort this problem out because the two saddest words in the English language are 'if only'. On a more positive note, if you do decide to get treatment you may find that you haven't actually left it too late to have children at all.

Helen Fielding, the author of *Bridget Jones's Diary,* had a baby at 43, Cherie Booth, Tony Blair's missus, had a baby at 45, the actresses Susan Sarandon (Louise) and Geena Davis (Thelma) gave birth at 46 and 47 respectively. So, never say never. Say *Arriba! Arriba! Arriba!*

My boyfriend ejaculates almost immediately during intercourse. Although he's good at other things in bed, I find the lack of sustained intercourse frustrating. Could his problem be related to the fact that he was circumcised as a child because his foreskin was too tight?

Sometimes it's easier to accept things if they can be explained away as illness or injury, but premature ejaculation is rarely a result of either. Occasionally it can be caused by urinary tract or prostate infections, or sometimes it can reflect more serious underlying health problems such as arteriosclerosis or neurological disorders.

In most cases, premature ejaculation is related to psycho-social issues. Some experts believe that boys who rush masturbation because they are afraid of being discovered, begin a pattern of rapid ejaculation that they can never subsequently break. In later life it can be triggered or aggravated by occupational stress, financial difficulties, family problems, guilt, sexual confusion or a lack of sexual and interpersonal skills. According to the Sexual Advice Association (SAA), a charitable organization that was set up to raise awareness, men who suffer from premature ejaculation tend to have more problematic relationships. A man may be with a partner who has unrealistic expectations or who is too sexually demanding, or feels dissatisfied with aspects of the relationship yet unable to communicate her concerns. An unsympathetic response intensifies anxiety which can lead to further failure.

The SAA runs a helpline. If your partner calls, they will help him to find a specialist in his area who will decide what treatment is appropriate. He may be advised to do both cognitive and behavioural therapy, a dual approach that tackles psychological concerns and teaches 'delay techniques' at the same time.

Delay techniques, such as the 'stop-start' or 'squeeze-release' masturbation methods, can help men to build up ejaculatory control, but in men who suffer from severe premature ejaculation these techniques don't translate into successful penetration. Your boyfriend may also be advised to try an anaesthetic cream or a delay spray. These products are constantly being improved and clinical trials of a spray which experts have high hopes for are currently under way. But unfortunately, because they work by decreasing sensation, they are not always popular. Prolong – a penile ring device which reduces sensitivity to delay ejaculation – works on the same basis.

The number of treatment options grows annually but, statistically, your boyfriend is unlikely to try any of them without your support. A survey by the Impotence Association has revealed that nine out of ten men suffering from sexual dysfunction never tell their GPs, even though 21 per cent of them blame it for the breakdown of their relationship and 62 per cent admit that it has had a negative effect on their self-esteem.

Since you don't have the glue of marriage or children to bind you together, your boyfriend's premature ejaculation

may feel too big a compromise for you to deal with.
But before you allow your frustrations to destroy this
relationship, remember that no one is perfect. The next guy
you get might be a god in the bedroom and a useless good-
for-nothing elsewhere. If your boyfriend is a great partner in
every 'other' way, maybe you should concentrate on 'other'
approaches to sex. There's a smorgasbord of delights that
don't include penetration. But if you want that, too, then
show him how to use a vibrator or get him to pump your
G-spot (two fingers curled about 5 cm/2 in in behind your
pubic bone, press behind your tummy button, as if to say
'come here').

Direct your sex life differently and you will alleviate the
performance pressure on him and hugely increase your
sexual satisfaction at the same time. In other words, if you
help him to help himself, you will be duly rewarded.

After orgasm I get cramp. It hurts me and penetration is painful for my husband. How can we resolve this problem?

If it hurt every time you coughed you would see your GP
straight away. Pain is always a sign that something is wrong
and the only way that you and your husband will be able to
resume physical relations is by finding out what is causing it.

A sympathetic female GP would be a good place to start,
but you might be better served by a family planning clinic.
You can find a clinic on the Family Planning Service website
or the Margaret Pyke Clinic in London is fantastic.

You could be suffering from any number of physical
conditions but once you begin to associate orgasm with
cramp, sex can become a trigger for pain. If you suspect
this might be the case, contact the Jane Wadsworth Clinic in
London. This NHS clinic offers fully integrated treatments
for all aspects of sexual health and sexual dysfunction.

Dr David Goldmeier, who runs the clinic, has had success treating cases such as yours using antispasmodics such as hyoscine (buscopan) before sex, but first you should get a pelvic ultrasound or MRI scan to exclude things such as fibroids. You could do this through your GP or find yourself – deep breath, clutch wallet – a private gynaecologist. Dib Datta, a consultant obstetrician and gynaecologist, says: 'GPs see themselves as gatekeepers to the NHS and have taken on a lot of the stuff that gynaecologists would have seen 20 years ago, but sometimes they are not well placed to answer the questions that are put to them.'

Gynaecological issues such as pelvic pain, painful intercourse or cramp at orgasm may destroy a woman's quality of life and even her relationship, but they are not generally life-threatening and that plays a part in how seriously they are taken on a limited NHS budget. As a result, finding the underlying cause, or achieving a definitive diagnosis can take years. According to a survey carried out by the Endometriosis All Party Parliamentary Group with Endometriosis UK, the average time between presenting at a GP's surgery with symptoms and a confirmed diagnosis of endometriosis is eight years.

That women are ostrich-like when it comes to gynaecological issues doesn't help. Figures from the NHS Cancer Screening Programme show that between 1995 and 2006 the number of women aged 25 to 29 who had taken a smear test had fallen 10 per cent. That's really disappointing when you consider that in 1988 when the screening programme was first introduced, the death rate from cervical cancer in women under 35 was among the highest in the developed world and now, more than 1,000 lives are saved each year.

At the end of the day we can hardly expect gynaecology to be a priority in the healthcare system if we don't prioritize it ourselves.

I am in my early fifties, happily married for over 20 years, yet I have rarely experienced orgasm. I do not get much physical sensation when ejaculating. In my younger days I experienced fellatio, but even then felt nothing. I doubt that I am unique, but literature on male sexual dysfunction does not document this phenomenon.

Put away the literature on male sexual dysfunction, pick up the phone and make an appointment with your doctor. Any number of underlying issues could be causing your inhibited sensitivity and inability to orgasm and you owe it to yourself and your penis to ensure that there is nothing physically wrong with you.

It is disturbing, but not particularly surprising, to think that you have tolerated this problem for the past 20 years without bothering to have a physical examination.

Male medical denial is universal and its consequences are universal, too. One man in nine will be diagnosed with prostate cancer, yet embarrassment means that few will have the easy and painless digital rectal examination and prostate specific antigen blood test to detect it. Women, facing similar odds of breast cancer, are much more likely to examine their breasts regularly and have a mammogram.

Men are at greater risk of stress-related illnesses than women. They are 30 per cent more likely than women to have a stroke before the age of 65 and it has been estimated that more than 3 million men have early type II diabetes, a disease with major complications, and don't know it.

On the other hand, if your lack of sensation has had so little impact on your happy marriage that you haven't been bothered enough to do anything about it, perhaps you should question whether there is any point in starting an investigation that might upset your happy apple cart.

Medical or psychological intervention into sexual dysfunction has a galling habit of shining light on precisely the things that one has either hidden subconsciously or would rather not see in the first place. And unfortunately, whether the diagnosis is illness, injury or emotional damage, the 'cure' generally requires wholesale commitment to something that might not be in the best interests of your otherwise happy and stable relationship – namely, change.

If you were deeply miserable with your wife I'd be the first to say 'go for it', but you clearly love her and she clearly loves you and, lets face it, no one gets through 20 years of marriage without a certain degree of sexual compatibility. So, it may just be that despite your letter, things are fine the way they are and despite your problem, you and your wife are completely sexually suited.

In many marriages sexual mismatching causes huge problems. One partner wants lots of sex, the other doesn't, and generally the only person who is satisfied is the lawyer.

If your wife's libido is lower than yours, she may well be perfectly satisfied with your existing sex life and you shouldn't discount this. Alternatively, if your wife is an absolute demon in the scratcher, over the past 20 years it is quite probable that her orgasm has taken precedence over your own less significant climax. If this is the case, she would obviously be loathe to change the present arrangements because she is used to having her needs 'on top', so to speak.

Either way, over two decades you and your wife have somehow managed to have a rewarding relationship and a functioning sex life. Since you are in your early fifties, I guess that your wife will hit menopause soonish and as you both head into your sixties and seventies it may be that the strength of your orgasm becomes less of a cause for consternation and your long and happy marriage becomes more of a cause for celebration.

When I make love with my girlfriend it causes her pain. She says the problem is that I'm too big. Are there any positions you can recommend that will make sex less sore?

Your girlfriend may be right about your size, but only about 10 per cent of men are so well endowed that it causes problems for their partners. In the 1950s, the great sex researcher Alfred Kinsey took measurements from 1,800 men and found that the average erection measured 15.6 cm (just over 6 in).

In 2001, Ansell, the maker of LifeStyles Condoms, set up private tents at the Daddy Rock night club in Cancun, Mexico, and over the course of a week qualified medical staff measured the erections of 300 male volunteers. They found the average length of an erect penis to be 14.8 cm (just under 6 in). (The smaller size reflects the fact that the measurements were taken by professionals; much of Kinsey's data was self-reported and studies suggest that men exaggerate the size of their erections by at least half a centimetre.) You can resolve this aspect of your query definitively by measuring your erection.

To do this you need to stand straight and use a piece of string to measure the upper side of your erection from the pubic bone to the tip. Put the string against a ruler and if the measurement falls between 14 cm and 16 cm (5½ in and 6 in), the pain your girlfriend is experiencing may relate to underlying medical conditions such as endometriosis, pelvic inflammatory disease or infection, and she should see her GP immediately.

Sex shouldn't hurt. The normal vagina can expand by up to 200 per cent during sex, so size is rarely an issue unless a woman isn't fully aroused. To accommodate an erect penis comfortably some women need up to 20 minutes of stimulation, so it may be that you and your girlfriend are rushing things. Are you skimping on foreplay? Provide enough manual and oral stimulation, paying particular attention to her clitoris and labia, and things may improve on their own.

You might want to try using lubricant for added slip and slide, but not as a short cut to arousal. When your girlfriend says she feels ready for penetration, spread more lubricant on to the head of your penis and around the vaginal opening, and then take things really slowly. The vaginal lips are incredibly sensitive and the longer you spend nuzzling your penis at the opening, the warmer the welcome that awaits you inside. Resist the temptation to thrust. Opt for a slow, sensual rhythm and stick to standard missionary position because it doesn't allow particularly deep penetration. Spoons is also a good option (you lie behind with your arms around her), and standing face to face will keep some distance between you, too.

If the problem you have really is caused by 'collision dyspareunia' – when your penis is so long that it hits her cervix – help is at hand in the form of a round rubber doughnut called the ComeClose protector ring. Designed by two women with well-endowed husbands, the device fits over the base of the penis to create a 2.5 cm (1 in) cushioned barrier between the two of you. Though it feels heavy, I'm assured that the added weight provides pleasurable pressure on the pelvis for both of you during sex. Does it work? I haven't tried it, but it's relatively inexpensive and if you weigh up the brownie points you'll get from your girlfriend for taking her problem seriously, it's a bargain.

20.

Contraceptives, KY, & genitourinary romance

I'm 22 and I have been on the combined Pill for two years since I got together with my boyfriend. I don't have any serious side-effects but I'm sick of ploughing my body with hormones. I can't believe that, in the long term, it is good for my health or my fertility. My boyfriend doesn't mind using condoms but are there any alternatives?

If men got pregnant, you can be damn sure that scientists would have produced a less invasive, more efficient form of contraception by now. But they don't. So women like you and me go through life chopping and changing from Pills to caps, to condoms to coils, in the vain hope that we will eventually find a simple sustainable form of contraception.

Easier said than done. My attempts at using the Pill resulted in a baby daughter, so I switched to the diaphragm. In theory, that should have worked but, in practice, it was so slippery and difficult to insert that when it pinged across the bathroom floor I often just left it there. Inevitably my haphazard approach caught up with me. Twins. Realizing that I wasn't cut out for any form of contraception that afforded a degree of human error, I had a coil inserted, but years of heavy periods later, I had it taken out.

Though I suspect that tinkering with hormones will eventually provide the answer, the constraints and side-effects of existing options make contraception a real drag. And because preventing pregnancy is considered a 'female issue', it doesn't get half the attention or financial backing that it really merits.

Think about it. Egyptian condoms didn't come in strawberry flavour but essentially we're still relying on a 2,000-year-old barrier method to protect us from sexually transmitted infections. And where is the male Pill? We've only been waiting 40 years. I know that there are a couple of options in development but don't hold your breath. It'll be another five years at least and, frankly, I can't see men queueing up for an implant of the female hormone progestogen which has to be supported by three-monthly testosterone injections to counter the 'feminizing effects' of man-breasts, a squeaky voice and a penchant for Manolos.

A second drug – NB-DNJ, which renders mice infertile after a three-week course of treatment – may turn out to be a revolutionary new rodent control but, if it is developed as a male Pill, women should bear in mind that it would have to be taken daily by a gender that struggles to remember events that occur once a year such as birthdays and anniversaries.

There is some light at the end of the tunnel. A range of microbicide gels are being developed in the UK, US and France which aims to provide protection against pregnancy and sexually transmitted infections. Carraguard, a seaweed gel that lines the cells of the vagina, is the most advanced. It works by putting a sticky coating around viruses and bacteria as they enter the vagina and, with the addition of a strong spermicide, it becomes a contraceptive, too. The second type of gel works by increasing acidity levels in the vagina to neutralize sperm – however, too much acid can burn the skin and cause lesions, which obviously makes infection more, rather than less, likely. The third option puts anti-retrovirals – HIV drugs – in a gel to prevent the virus replicating, or to render it non-infectious.

That's the good news. The bad news is that none of them really works yet. At the moment they're about 50 per cent effective but, even at that level, mathematical models show that if a small proportion of women in lower-income countries used a 60 per cent effective microbicide in half their unprotected sexual encounters, 2 million HIV infections could be averted over three years.

Though microbicides offer hope of a contraceptive alternative to condoms which will also protect women against sexually transmitted infections (STIs) and HIV, unfortunately because the main beneficiaries would be poor women who can't afford to pay for the products, finding funding is akin to drawing blood from a stone.

Can I take the morning-after pill more than once a month, and how safe is it? I've taken it about five or six times in my life and once this month already. Whenever I buy it the pharmacist asks personal questions in front of everyone, making me feel like a naughty teenager.

The morning-after pill is effective only up to 72 hours after intercourse but the level of protection declines dramatically during that time. In the first 24 hours it prevents 95 per cent of pregnancies, but that figure drops to 85 per cent within the next 24 hours and only 58 per cent if taken after that. Using the morning-after pill twice in one month does suggest that you ought to be investigating a more reliable form of contraception and that you have not used a condom means that you may have exposed yourself to STIs. However, in terms of safety, there is no medical evidence to indicate that taking it more than once in a cycle will cause you any long-term health problems.

Our own Dr Mark Porter describes it as 'incredibly safe', though he emphasizes the need for other forms of contraception. That said, the morning-after pill can disrupt the regularity of your menstrual cycle, and since getting your period is your main way of knowing whether you are pregnant or not, using it more than once in a month can increase your level of uncertainty until your period arrives.

The majority of over-the-counter sales of the morning-after pill are to responsible mid-twenties urban professionals who don't want to run the risk of an unplanned pregnancy. Before they are given the tablet, most of them are grilled about their sexual behaviour and are usually advised to go on the Pill. Many women avoid the Pill because it doesn't agree with them or makes them gain weight, while single women question the validity of pumping themselves full of hormones on the off chance that they will have sex, at some point in the future, with a man they have yet to meet. Bar condoms, which have a 15 per cent failure rate because of product defects and user errors, intrauterine devices (IUDs) provide the only hormone-free method of contraception, but they are painful to insert and remove, and can make periods heavier and more painful.

The complexity of existing contraceptive options helps to explain why one in every three women in Britain has a termination before the age of 45. Ann Furedi, of the British Pregnancy Advisory Service (BPAS), says that 'for women who are not in a relationship, the morning-after pill is even safer than the contraceptive pill because it is only an occasional dose of hormones, although obviously it doesn't protect against STIs'. The BPAS states that 'there is no limit' to how many times you can use it.

Because time is crucial to the effectiveness of the morning-after pill the Family Planning Association (FPA) believes that women should be encouraged to keep emergency contraception in the same way that people keep a supply of paracetamol or antihistamines. An FPA survey revealed that although 75 per cent of women would like to have emergency pills in advance, more than 80 per cent did not know they could ask for this. After the FPA survey there was concern from MPs and religious groups about how availability might encourage unprotected sex, but in 2007 a review by the emergency contraception experts James Trussell and Elizabeth G. Raymond reported that 'evidence would seem to demonstrate convincingly that making emergency contraception pills more widely available does not increase risk-taking or adversely affect regular contraceptive use' and that 'women who are the most diligent about ongoing contraceptive use are those most likely to seek emergency treatment'.

You have used emergency contraception only five or six times. If this incident heralds the start of a new relationship then consider the long-term options, but if it is a one-off, you can buy the morning-after pill in advance from some pharmacies. The pills are sold in packs of one, two or three. They are not cheap, but peace of mind is priceless.

My wife and I recently had sex in a bubble bath. It was wonderful, but she developed a bad case of thrush soon after. Can we blame the bubble bath?

Sex in the bath is usually a rather gymnastic and uncomfortable exchange, and a strangely dry affair. Water washes away any natural lubrication, which increases the level of friction during penetration. This can irritate the delicate tissue in the vagina, making it more susceptible to thrush.

The secret to good underwater sex is lots and lots of lube. Water-based products, such as KY Jelly, are no good because they wash off. But silicone, a synthetic substance, which is not water soluble, retains its slippery properties making it ideal for extended intercourse and underwater sex. Silicone is not absorbed by the skin and rarely causes any kind of reaction; in fact, some brands, such as Sliquid Ride, advertise themselves as being 100 per cent vegan friendly, non-toxic, free of hypoallergenics, glycerin and parabens.

Your wife could also try Yes Oil, a lubricant containing two rich organic butters – cocoa and shea – which impart smoothness and body; two emollient oils – organic sweet almond and sunflower – which confer a silky texture while also moisturizing the skin; and, lastly, a little white organic bees' wax and some vitamin E which, as well as benefiting the skin, acts as a preservative.

Thrush affects three out of every four women at some point in their lives and the UK's thrush treatment market is worth about £18 million a year. However, much of that is misspent because the symptoms of thrush are the same as the symptoms of a host of other skin conditions, such as eczema or lichen sclerosis, which need to be treated with topical steroids rather than anti-fungals.

If your wife gets repeated bouts of thrush, she should make an appointment with her GP so that she gets an accurate diagnosis. If it does turn out to be thrush, you also must get checked out because men get it too and you could be reinfecting each other.

Standard advice to women who want to avoid thrush is to wear cotton underwear and avoid tight trousers, antibiotics, vaginal deodorants, penetrative sex, perfumed bubble baths, pentrative sex in perfumed bubble baths, etc, etc. More recently, doctors in the know have begun to advise women to try using all cotton tampons, too. Though brands such as Natracare are more expensive than other tampons, it stands to reason that the polypropylene, perfume and bleach in normal rayon, viscose and plastic sanitary products will irritate the delicate membranes in the vulva more than a natural fibre.

Similarly, think twice about what you put in your bath. The detergents involved in making scented bubbles have caused so many adverse reactions that children's bubble baths in the US must carry a warning advising that prolonged use can cause skin irritation and urinary tract infections.

We all love bubble baths, but when you and your wife next think of getting it on in the tub, add a few drops of ylang-ylang to an almond oil base instead.

I want to take my new beau to be screened for sexual health. But he says it's not very romantic and that I should trust him when he says he's 'clean'. What should I do?

He's right. Having a test is not exactly romantic. But nor is finding out that you are one of the 83,745 people in the UK that has genital warts. And, compared with genital herpes, testing is a walk in the park.

Contagious oozing blisters anyone? Nope, not very romantic at all. Mind you, four out of five people who have the herpes virus don't exhibit noticeable symptoms, so they just pass it on to suckers who don't understand the importance of sexual health screening. It's why the incidence of genital herpes continues to rise; 16 per cent in girls aged between 16 and 19.

Infertility isn't very romantic either, but chlamydia is still winning prizes for 'the most commonly treated sexually transmitted disease in the UK'. One young adult in ten screened through the 2006 National Chlamydia Screening Programme tested positive for the symptomless infection that can scupper a woman's chances of having a child.

And what about death, eh? Aids has been written off as a medical condition that affects gay men, drug addicts and immigrants, but in the UK heterosexual transmission of HIV now exceeds any other source. There were nearly 8,000 new cases of HIV in the UK in one year, while it is estimated to be undiagnosed in a further 21,600 people. At least 18,000 people have died of Aids in Britain already, and although anti-retrovirals can delay death, they don't cure the condition.

So, romantic is relative. But trust is not. Sexually transmitted infections (STIs) have reached such epidemic proportions in our population that no one can consider themself 'clean' unless they have the test results to prove it.

If your beau is embarrassed about going to a genitourinary medicine (GUM) clinic, get him to do it through DrThom, the online sexual health clinic. It is the only online medical service registered with the Healthcare Commission, and the 'Silver Screening' package for men and women tests for genital chlamydia, genital gonorrhoea or HIV. All he has to do is to register online, make his payment and then wait for the innocuous-looking testing pack to arrive in the post. The tests are idiot proof.

For the chlamydia and gonorrhoea tests, your beau needs to collect a urine sample and the HIV test requires a saliva sample. However, the HIV test is unlikely to be able to detect signs of HIV infection if it occurred within the past three and a half months, but this is the same if you have an HIV test at a GUM clinic.

Once he has collected his samples he posts them off to the laboratory. Three to five days later DrThom will send a text message to his mobile telling him to log on to the website to collect his results. If there is any uncertainty as to what the results are, DrThom will ask for a telephone number to call him on. The service is confidential and his GP will not be informed of his results without his permission.

DrThom's 'Silver Screening' package comes with a price tag. If your beau was less of a chicken he could get all those tests free at his local GUM clinic. And then he could use the money to take you out for dinner instead. Now that is romantic.

21.

Age, expectations & dancing naked in the Himalayas with lesbian sheep farmers

I'm a widower and over 90, but I still masturbate regularly. Could this be harmful to me in any way? Does it have any health benefits?

George Burns once said that 'sex at age 90 is like trying to shoot pool with a rope'. Masturbation, on the other hand, is a much more reliable form of release.

You don't have to get dressed up for it and there is little chance of your right hand crying off with a headache or complaining that you take too long. The only downside is that sex with yourself can become a little predictable.

However, the addition of a little lube can alter the sensation dramatically. If you can't get Astroglide or KY Jelly, Johnson's Baby Oil gel is a good and inexpensive alternative. Available in any supermarket or pharmacy, baby oil gel is smoother than Vaseline but washes off easily, particularly if you add a little conventional baby oil to the mix.

You might also consider some sound effects. Masturbation is something that men and women usually do in secret, so it is often executed in silence. If you live alone, you might find it liberating to make a bit of noise and an operatic soundtrack can also enhance the experience. Masturbation generally conjures up images of furtive teenagers and sticky magazines, but it is a lifetime practice that can fill a sexual gap at any age. It is still a surprisingly taboo subject, particularly for someone of your age, so it is difficult to estimate the number of elderly men who practise it regularly. Sex studies rarely include people over 60 because the presumption is that sexual interest tails off. However, a 1987 study published in the *Archives of Sexual Behavior,* which evaluated the sexual behavior of 81 healthy married men aged 60 to 71 (34 men aged 60 to 65 years and 47 aged 66 to 71 years), found that although there was a decline in sexual intercourse, half of the men reported masturbating regularly.

Although your fears about the dangers of masturbating are groundless, they are very common. There are symbolic associations between sex and death – the French word for orgasm, *petit mort* means literally 'the little death' – and the possibility of heart attack or stroke during orgasm discourages some.

In fact, far from being harmful, your penchant for self-soothing may be the reason that you are still going strong at 90+. A 1997 study published in the *British Medical Journal* found that men who had fewer orgasms were twice as likely to die as those having two or more orgasms a week. The ten-year analysis of 918 men aged 45 to 59 from the town of Caerphilly in South Wales was followed up in 2001 with a study, more specifically, on cardiovascular health. It found that having sex three or more times a week was associated with a 50 per cent reduction in the risk of heart attack or stroke. The Caerphilly results are so persuasive that the current British Heart Foundation advertising campaign features an elderly couple kissing and a list of ways in which they can keep fit, one of which is sex.

Besides the fact that having orgasms helps to protect your heart, it also releases tension (unlike relationships which often just cause it) and increases the levels of serotonin 'the feel-good' chemical in the brain. This leaves you feeling happier, more relaxed, and better able to sleep. Woody Allen put it in a nutshell when he said: 'Masturbation, don't knock it. It's sex with someone you love.'

My wife and I are over 80 and sexually active. Our orgasms are very strong and we wondered whether this might be putting pressure on our hearts. Is this so?

Hell, no. While many 80-year-olds are limiting themselves to eating, breathing and making it to the bathroom on a Zimmer frame, you and your wife are increasing your stamina, losing weight and strengthening all your muscles (the heart is a muscle, remember) simply by enjoying regular sessions of the only palatable form of exercise known to man or woman – horizontal jogging.

The relationship between sex and heart attacks can largely be blamed on the former US Vice-President Nelson Rockefeller, who died on top of his mistress, 27-year-old Megan Marshak, on 26 January 1979. Though the risk is higher if, like Rockefeller, the sex is adulterous, in reality, only 1 per cent of heart attacks are triggered by sexual activity. That's a negligible statistic at any age, but it is surely even less relevant to a man who has exceeded the average lifespan of a British male by at least five years.

Contrary to your concerns, evidence suggests that regular orgasm might extend your life (see previous question). Any activity that burns calories helps to keep you fit. Dr Jay Lee, a Canadian urologist, uses golf analogies to illustrate the energy expended during sex. For men, he says that an average round of sexual intercourse equates to 'a game of golf, carrying your own clubs'. He suggests that the workout potential for a woman can range from 'a challenging 18-hole course with hills to sitting in the golf cart drinking iced tea.'

Besides keeping you fit and healthy, sex protects against prostate cancer, lowers blood pressure and is a marvellous way of dodging depression and aches and pains.

So, all you really need to know is that not only is sex good, it is good for you.

———————

I'm 65 and my wife and I have been married for 42 years. When we were young, sex was limited because she didn't like the Pill and we were worried about her getting pregnant. As the kids got older we stopped having sex – it was never really her thing and I kept my urges under control. But I'm getting old and feel as if I have lived my whole life for the family. My wife would have a heart attack if I suggested sex now. I look at us sitting in silence and think is this all there is? Will I ever feel passion or excitement again?

At 65, you are probably coming to the end of your professional life. When life expectancy was shorter, retirement was a question of 'what am I capable of doing?', but better health care means that retirees can now afford to ask themselves 'What do I want to do?', and invariably, that question involves addressing relationships. Rather than try and change their life, many men simply decide to change their wife and despite an overall decline in the UK divorce rate, the rate for people over sixty has actually increased.

In the short term, newly divorced men probably do experience a sense of renewal, but because they are more set in their ways, less flexible and less accommodating, any subsequent marriages are statistically more likely fail. Physical factors such as declining vision, hearing or mobility impose social limitations on the elderly, and men who walk out on long-term marriages are also sacrificing friends, family and their existing social support group just as they are about to need it most.

Quality of life has been defined as 'the extent to which our hopes and ambitions are matched by experience'. Feelings of disappointment about ambitions which have not been realized, or experiences, such as marriage, which have not lived up to expectations, are compounded by the realization that there is very little time left in which to change those outcomes. It is a matter for regret that the issues which have undermined your marriage were not addressed earlier, because so much could have been done to help. Dr David Goldmeier, Clinical Lead for the Jane Wadsworth Sexual Function Clinic says that 'once a couple stop having sex, even for a few months, they slip into "non-sexual relationship mode" where it becomes very difficult to initiate sex. They, in effect, become platonic partners in a conspiracy of silence.'

In her book *The Dangerous Old Woman*, psychoanalyst Clarissa Pinkola Estés says 'Just because a woman is silent does not mean she agrees…' Similarly, just because a woman does not want to have sex with her husband, does not mean she does not want to have sex. To break the silence between you, you need to acknowledge your feelings and talk to your wife. And then you need to get professional help. Dr Goldmeier's clinic at St Mary's Hospital would assess you both to establish whether your wife is suffering from low desire and might benefit from oestrogen cream or even HRT. Treatment would be supported with mindfulness meditation leading to formal sex therapy, so that you could both learn how to 'be in the physical/sexual moment in a non judgemental way.'

And there is a lot you can do to help yourselves. John W. Osborne, Ph.D Professor Emeritus, University of Alberta suggests that you read David Schnark's book *Constructing the Sexual Crucible*, because 'he does not put age limits on sexual behaviour and provides several case studies of couples who rediscovered the joys of sex in later life.'

The prospect of becoming an old person in a society

which ignores the elderly is daunting – Age Concern says that one in four older people over the age of 65 in the UK is clinically depressed – but the place you find yourself in at 65 is governed by millions of decisions that you did, or did not make in your life, and it is only when you have accepted responsibility for those choices and created some meaning from your past that you will come to terms with who you are now, and what lies ahead for you.

If you view the years to come as a chance to make the most of yourself, to invest in your intellect and nourish the relationships that have sustained you, getting older has the potential to be the most progressive, fruitful and intimate stage of your life and your relationship.

I'm 70 and lonely after my wife died, as I haven't found another woman. As gay men seem now to be quite accepted, is it too late to become a homosexual?

Carpe diem. It's never too late to try anything, sweetie. If you have a beating heart, lung function and a credit card, you can dance naked in the Himalayas with lesbian sheep farmers and bugger the begrudgers.

Being bi-curious is much more common than you might think. In 1993 a team at the Harvard School of Public Health found that 8.7 per cent of the men they questioned reported feeling some same-sex attraction but were not engaging in homosexual behaviour. In the UK the National Survey of Sexual Attitudes and Lifestyles in 2000 echoed those figures; 8.1 per cent of men that were questioned had felt a sexual attraction towards the same sex at least once in their lives but had never acted on it.

When you were growing up in the 1940s and 1950s, homosexuality was illegal, so exploring that aspect of your sexuality would have been risky, to say the least.

Although the law prohibits discrimination against homosexuals, and being gay has, as you say, become 'quite accepted', you probably shouldn't broadcast your change of direction to your friends and family as they may feel it is insensitive to the memory of your wife. They may also worry about your health. The spread of Aids has been contained in the UK by safe sex campaigns and the development of anti-retroviral drugs but everyone, male or female, gay or straight, should use a condom when having sex. I'd also recommend that you take things slowly and use lots of lubricant.

The fact that you are 70 will be no barrier to meeting a partner. Older men are greatly in demand on the gay scene and there are several dating websites such as Silver Daddies and Nice Daddies, which are dedicated to the more mature gay male. If you can get past the photos of naked men showing off their tackle to scroll through to the entries you will almost certainly find a few like-minded individuals.

Internet dating makes meeting men a lot easier but you should always exercise caution when making contact. Never use your own email address; don't give out personal information or money; always meet in a public place; tell a friend where you are going; take a mobile phone; don't go to your home or his home; and don't take a lift.

Though homosexuality is slightly more complicated in terms of social acceptance, don't be put off. Seize the day while you can because life is too short. It whizzes by in the blink of an eye and we should all, each and every one of us, be doing our damnedest to ensure that we have no regrets when we blow out the candles on our 90th birthday cake. Or our 70th. Or our 40th. No one ever dies wishing they had done less with their life, but many people do regret failing to chase their dreams, or explore their sexuality. Good luck, sir.

Resources

AGEING

Ageing in America
Issues related to aging and seniors, in the United States. *www.ageinginamerica.com*

Council on the Ageing
COTA is Australia's leading seniors' organization, with individual members and seniors organization members in all States and Territories. *www.cota.org.au*

SAGA
Everything for the over fifties and then some. *www.saga.co.uk*

COUNSELLING & THERAPY

British Association for Behavioural and Cognitive Psychotherapies
www.babcp.com

British Association for Counselling and Psychotherapy *www.bacp.co.uk*

College of Sexual and Relationship Therapists *www.cosrt.org.uk*

Gottman Relationship Institute
www.gottman.com

Institute of Psychosexual Medicine
www.ipm.org.uk

No Panic *www.nopanic.org.uk*

OCD Action *www.ocdaction.org.uk*

Paula Hall Sexual psychotherapist
www.paulahall.co.uk

The Priory Hospital, North London
OCD Clinic *www.priorygroup.com*

Sex Addicts Anonymous *www.sexaa.org*

Theravive *www.theravive.com*

DATING & SINGLES HOLIDAYS

Events4singles *www.events4singles.com*

Exodus Travel *www.exodus.co.uk*

Grapevine Social
www.grapevinesocial.com

Nice Daddies *www.nicedaddies.com*

Saga Holidays *www.sagaholidays.com*

The Senior Dating Group USA
www.seniordatinggroup.com

Silver Daddies *www.silverdaddies.com*

Singles on the Go
www.singlesonthego.com

Solo Travel Online
www.solotravelonline.com

FEMALE HEALTH

Betty Dodson's Sex Boutique
www.dodsonandross.com/boutique

British Pregnancy Advisory Service
www.bpas.org

Dr. Laura Berman
America's leading expert in female sexual health. *www.drlauraberman.com*

Endometriosis UK
www.endometriosis-uk.org

Family Planning Association
www.fpa.org.uk

Good To Know Diets
Menopause diet plant
www.goodtoknow.co.uk/diet/268782/The-menopause-dietplan

Kegel exercises *www.natural-woman.com*

Margaret Pyke Centre
www.margaretpyke.org

Win Health Pelvic floor exerciser
www.win-health.co.uk/pfx-pelvic-floor-exerciser-biofeedback.html

FETISH

Alter Ego North America's longest running and best attended monthly fetish party, in Ft. Lauderdale USA. *www.usafetishparty.com*

Breathless *www.breathless.uk.com*

FetLife Free social network for the BDSM community.
www.fetlife.com

Fur Affinity *www.furaffinity.net*

Fur Suit Sex *www.fursuitsex.com*

Informed Consent
BDSM web boards and listings.
www.informedconsent.co.uk

Shoecraft Fetish Footwear
www.shoecraft.com.au

Torture Garden *www.torturegarden.com*

Tribalectic
http://community.tribalectic.com

UK Fur *www.ukfur.org*

Wellie-Web *www.wellie-web.co.uk*

GENDER & SEXUALITY

Straightguise
www.straightguise.com

The Women of the Beaumont Society
www.gender.org.uk/wobsmatters

Gay counselling in the United States of America *www.gaycounselling.org*

MALE HEALTH

American Prostate Society
www.americanprostatesociety.com

Andrology Australia
www.andrologyaustralia.org

Health Advice Men Only
www.healthadvicemenonly.com

Male Health *www.malehealth.co.uk*

Prostate Cancer Charity
Helpline staffed by urological nurses who can provide information and support regarding prostate cancer.
www.prostate-cancer.org.uk

MARRIAGE & RELATIONSHIP COUNSELLING

Relate *www.relate.org.uk*

Sexual Health Australia
www.sexualhealthaustralia.com.au

Tavistock Centre for Couple Relationships *www.tccr.org.uk*

SEXUAL DYSFUNCTION

Advanced Medical Institute
Treatment for female sexual dysfunction.
www.amiaustralia.com.au

British Association for Sexual and Relationship Therapy *www.basrt.org.uk*

Jane Wadsworth Clinic
www.imperial.nhs.uk/thejefferisswing/index.htm

Sexual Dysfunction Association
Formerly the Impotence Association
www.sda.uk.net

SEXUAL HEALTH

DrThom Online GP and sexual health clinic. *www.drthom.com*

NHS Direct *www.nhsdirect.nhs.uk*

Planned Parenthood Federation of America *www.plannedparenthood.org*

Sexual Advice Association
www.sda.uk.net

Sexual Health and Family Planning Australia *www.shfpa.org.au*

Sexual health information
Online guide to facts on sexual health screening, contraception and STIs.
www.bbc.co.uk/health/physical_health/sexual_health

Society of Sexual Health Advisers
www.ssha.info

SEX TOYS, LUBRICANTS & ACCESSORIES

Agent Provocateur
www.agentprovocateur.com

Ann Summers
www.annsummers.com

British Condoms
www.britishcondoms.co.uk

ComeClose Protector Ring
www.comeclose.co.uk

Good Vibrations
www.goodvibes.com

Jimmyjane *www.jimmyjane.com*

Lovehoney *www.lovehoney.co.uk*

Pjur USA *www.pjurusa.com*

Temptations
www.temptationsdirect.co.uk

Yes Oil Lubricants
www.yesyesyes.org

OTHER USEFUL RESOURCES

Estronaut Coital alignment technique
www.estronaut.com/a/coital_align_technique.htm

Nerve Online database for dating and sexual advice.
www.nerve.com

The New York Laser Clinic
Laser hair removal in London.
www.thenewyorklaserclinic.co.uk

Vegan Porn *www.veganporn.com*

The Vegan Society
www.vegansociety.com

Voyeur Web Porn
www.voyeurweb.com

Index

218

224